Encountering:
the handiwork of faith

Rev. Shirley Heeg

ENCOURAGEMENT

Dr. James Cook, my seminary professor and friend, wrote me many letters through the years. I've included a couple of excerpts below although I have second thoughts because they seem overly complimentary. Still, I wanted to do more than list his name here as a thank you. Letters expose our hearts and these words are "pure" Jim and Jean, enthusiasm and all. Such encouragers! I am grateful to have known them.

Dear Shirley,   March 20, 1992
    Thanks for the "Heart to Hart" piece. I read it to Jean at breakfast this am & she responded with – "That's just not <u>like</u> the other pieces other ministers write in their newsletters!" I agree. It's pure Shirley Heeg! – and that always means <u>special quality</u>!
…Jean joins me in sending our love. Greetings to John and your children!   Jim

Dear Shirley –   May 5, 1997
    The May issue of <u>Encounter</u> reminded me that you have lost none of your literary eloquence… <u>Wow</u>! You just toss off images most of us would die for! Through your remarkable gifts of observation and language – God's grace & peace do put a spring in my step! <u>Thanks</u>!
    …I hope that both your congregation and your wonderful children are giving you abundant love and joy to more than balance the woes….
                                                       Jim

~ Dr. James I. Cook ~
(1925-2007)
I thank my God every time I remember you. (Philippians 1:3)

INTRODUCTION

Writing this first letter was like sending a postcard from a road trip we had just begun. We knew Ferry Memorial Church families well and had spent many hours with them, not only on church boards and committees but also eating at their homes, raising our children together, and sharing our losses and our dreams. Now we were leaving them to start another adventure on our own.

November, 1991
Dear friends at Ferry,

This past week I began my ministry as the pastor of Hart Congregational United Church of Christ. In just three short days I've shaken dozens of hands, heard names I couldn't recall a moment later, and poured over the church directory with a map of Hart on my lap. The church has 137 communing members and a Sunday School of between 50 and 75 children. Sunday, after our first service together, we had a coffee hour chuck full of balloons, cake, and smiles. The Sunday School had practiced a song to welcome me and that was another fun surprise! Anyone who might look at this week in my planning calendar would think I'd been scheduling meetings and projects around here for ages, but I still feel brand new! Amid these beginnings and endings, I wanted to send this description "home" to Ferry Memorial because so many of you have asked.

Hart UCC is located just a few blocks south of the business district on State Street, the main street of Hart. The building is over a hundred years old, much like your Heritage Hall. I think it's a beautiful place to worship, with red and gold carpet and a gracious parlor at the back of its long narrow sanctuary. The acoustics are especially clear because of the dome at the front and the plaster walls and ceiling. It has stained glass windows and a lovely old organ. My office is in the parish house which also holds Sunday School rooms. Between this and the sanctuary is another building where the Sunday School holds opening singing and which houses a preschool program during the week.

I know Hart isn't exactly on the beaten path for most of you, but if you do have an occasion to come north, please know you have an invitation to drop in. …You are where this most recent change in our lives started. John and I and our children will miss you.

God's peace to you all!
Shirley

October 15, 1991
Hart Congregational United Church of Christ
Pastoral Search Committee
408 State Street
Hart, Michigan 40420

Dear friends

The confidence and hope expressed in your manner toward me and in the extension of the call to be your pastor have meant a great deal to me. In the denomination with which I am most familiar, the response to such a call is communicated personally as well as signified by the signing of a contract, Therefore, I'm writing to confirm that, with joyful anticipation, I am accepting your call to serve our Lord as pastor of the Hart Congregational United Church of Christ. May God bless our time together.

Grace and Peace,
Shirley Heeg

Announcing...
This congregation and the West Michigan Association of the United Church of Christ announce the installation of Rev. Shirley Heeg on December 8, 1991, 4 pm. Pastors of the sixteen churches in this association as well as participants from HUCC and other area churches will lead the worship. Please plan to come so we can celebrate this new beginning together. A luncheon will follow the service

The Herald-Journal / Dec. 5, 1991

Hart Congregational Church to install pastor this Sunday in special afternoon service

The Hart Congregational United Church of Christ will install the Rev. Shirley Heeg as its pastor during an afternoon worship service this Sunday, Dec. 8 at 4 p.m. The community is invited.

Rev. Heeg, of Benona Township, began as minister of the church Nov. 1. The congregation extended the call to her in late September. Rev. Heeg replaces Rev. Walter Noffke who retired.

Rev. Heeg earned a Bachelor of Arts in English, mathematics and teaching certificate from Grand Valley State University in 1968 and continued her education with 29 hours of graduate work in English at Michigan State University in 1969 and 1970, and seven hours of New Testament Greek at Hope College in 1985-86. She earned a Masters in Christian Education in 1989 and a Masters in Divinity in 1991, both from Western Theological Seminary in Holland.

With the New Era Reformed Church, Rev. Heeg was involved in teaching and worship design in 1990-91. She was a substitute teacher in Occana and Newaygo schools in 1987-88 and designed a summer creative writing program for the Shelby Public Library in 1984-85. She was a high school English teacher with the Shelby schools from 1970-76 and taught junior high English at Jenison Public Schools in 1968-69.

Rev. Heeg entered her theological training while raising a family. She and her husband John have four children, Merileigh, Aaron, Anne and Elyse.

The call to Rev. Heeg capped a year-long church process of self-study which included assessing strengths, weaknesses, areas of concern and goals.

Rev. Heeg was ordained as Minister of the Word, by the Muskegon Classis, Reformed Church in American, on Oct. 29 at the Ferry Memorial Reformed Church in Montague.

Rev. Shirley Heeg

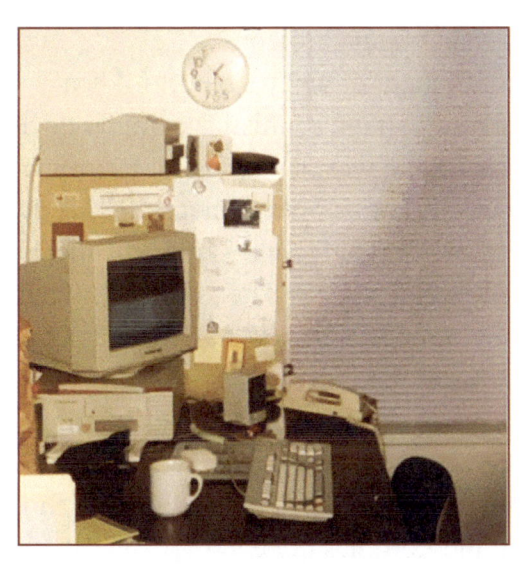

ENCOUNTER

The newsletter at HUCC was called the *Encounter*. I liked that name as soon as I heard it. Faith has always been relational for me, both with others and with God. Much is possible whenever we meet and connect.

I titled my articles "Heart to Hart" because Dr. James Cook had chosen that phrase as the theme of his homily when he gave the "Charge to the Pastor" at my ordination. I soon realized that his words were more than clever. They would shape my commitment as I began to entrust myself to these people whom I barely knew, who, in turn, were also trusting the process, trusting God, and beginning to trust me.

Encounter, November 1991
"Heart to Hart" from the Pastor…
*Encounter (en koun' ter) - verb, to meet unexpectedly, come upon

     This morning the storm door banged soundly behind my children when they raced off as usual to catch their school bus, but a moment later I was surprised to hear one of them twisting the knob again. "Come, look, Mom," she begged. "You can see the moon, a bright star, and the sunrise – all in the same sky!" I walked out into the cold, clear morning air to see a crescent moon etched into the dark taupe sky and, not far from it, the glint of one star. No doubt they were reflecting the first rays of a sunrise yet promised by the mauve and orange horizon.

Standing there, I thought of a news report I'd heard just recently. Scientists are now using a sophisticated radar device to intently search the sky for radio waves, hoping to determine if there are other intelligent life forms in the universe. This device scans innumerable frequencies rapidly and systematically, but can only focus on one small area at a time. The astronomer had compared this to looking through a straw. As I looked out at the remarkable morning lights around me, I couldn't help but wonder about another comparison. Although new life dawns, filling the sky with its message, how many still await the vision, and vainly search for it with straws? We, too, like eager children, can invite them, "Come, see what the Lord has done!"

Grace and Peace,
Pastor Shirley

December, 1991, Christmas Letter
Dear friends,

I'm writing this as we approach the third Sunday of Advent, traditionally the time the church celebrates our joy at the coming of our savior, Jesus Christ. It seems good to write to you with joy on my mind because that's what's in my heart as well! In the past year, John and I and our children have talked, prayed, and wondered much about God's leading as I left seminary and sought a church to serve. One of my first impressions of this congregation was that those on the ministerial search committee genuinely enjoyed one another and that made being with them a refreshing experience! Since then I've seen the sparkle of joy in the eyes of children here, joy in the faces of the choir as they practice and sing, joy in your faces as you reach out to shake my hand or hug me. That welcome has been a beautiful gift to my family and myself and we appreciate it deeply.

In my visiting and phoning, I'm just beginning to sketch some details into my picture of who you really are: your life experiences, your hopes and dreams, your caring for others, and your faith which permeates all of the above. I've heard stories of personal struggles, but also always of hope and joy. This place, like no other I've ever known, radiates anticipation. What a blessed place to spend Advent, to approach a new year, to begin a ministry!

So this Christmas we feel we've already been blessed by God with the warmth of a new "family." We join you in looking forward realistically to both challenges and joys in the year ahead. It's our prayer that together our lives may more and more fully express the compassion, justice, and truth of our Lord.

We love you all.
Pastor Shirley, John, Elyse, Anne, Aaron, and Merileigh

Encounter, December 1991
"Heart to Hart" from the Pastor…

"What do you want for Christmas?" It's a familiar question to all of us and, very likely, one you've both asked and answered at some time in the past month as I have. Yet, it's always a question that makes me stop and think for a while before I answer. I find I consider who is asking – whether my father, my husband, or my youngest child – because that makes a difference how I will answer. And when I'm doing the asking, I know from experience that I'll have to be willing to be flexible and open to what I will hear. (I love to shop in department stores and specialty shops, but John's list often sends me to the hardware or a farm supply warehouse!) As always, there are also things I'd love for others to have, but which I cannot give them by myself. These things come to mind as I think of you today.

For those who face the first Christmas after the death of someone deeply loved, I would want a love that spreads to fill the empty spaces, that comforts in sorrow, that opens our hearts once again to receive unexpected blessings from God and assures us that temporal and eternal life are inseparable.

For teens challenging themselves and the world, I would want a fair chance, sharp-thinking minds that aren't easily fooled, goodness and straight answers from those who teach and love them, and a feel for consequences when making decisions. In other words: the way, the truth, and the life found in Jesus. And one more thing – the key to it all – friendship, ours and God's.

For husbands and wives who are so busy shouldering responsibilities, debts, and decisions that they find their love for each other growing cold, I would want "together" time, holding hands and talking, "being" together, and not just doing. I would want warmth and tenderness, sharing and trusting. I would want them to see their love as God's blessing, as sacred gift.

For children who look up to us, I would want our eyes to meet and our hands to clasp. I would want laps for sitting on and times of listening. I would want stories of family, of God's family, of belonging and being important, of being cherished. I would want good hugs.

For those who are struggling with pain, with life, with loneliness, I would want peace and hope and deep connectedness with another, with the Other who loves without limits, who never turns away, who can be counted on. I would want new closeness with God as they go on, so they can go on.

What I want most of all for others (and for myself as well) is what we are all about here in the church. It's why I'm in the church. It's what God gives at Christmas. Have a meaningful, holy holiday!

Grace and Peace,
Pastor Shirley

[January 1992 missing]

                      Encounter, February 1992
"Heart to Hart" from the Pastor...thoughts on hearing

"Did you hear that?" The words are almost spoken with emphasis, whether whispered in apprehension after an unknown sound wakes you from your sleep, in disbelief that someone could have said such a thing, or in delight as at the first gurgled "mama" of a child. Sometimes it's a sound that we didn't expect. "Did you hear that?"

Hearing is technical. Sound waves impact our eardrum and cause it to vibrate. Nerve endings transmit signals to our brain for interpretation. (We've all made and labeled the drawings in school!) And yet, hearing can also be much more.

To hear is to take something inside of ourselves. It's struggling to understand. And our impulse, when we hear, is to call others into the room and wait with them in suspended silence until..."There! There it is again!" When we hear the frightening night sound, we want to touch someone, to reassure ourselves that we are not alone. When we hear the unthinkable, the astounding, we draw it to another's attention to check if we have understood clearly. The hearing of discovery makes us marvel and wonder. "Have others experienced this?" we ask ourselves.

We come to church to hear the Word of God. We don't primarily "see" that word, except with the eye of the ear, the eye of our mind. There we enter into a strange land where bushes burn and are not consumed, sun-tanned men repair heavy fishing nets, or the world's very first rainbow arches serenely after a long storm. Yet, we are transported into this reality by words. Just words – sounds and breath. Strange, isn't it, that in this age of advancements in lighting and special effects, of sophisticated entertainment and marketing, that the church still gathers to hear the stories, letters, and poetry of an ancient, middle-eastern, nomadic tribe read aloud to us? We have inherited an oral tradition; long before they were ever written, these words were spoken aloud to generations of hearers who gathered around campfires, altars, holy mountains, temples, common tables, and wooden crosses.

    It is, after all, the word of our God – sacred word. In the beginning God created the world with a word. The word became flesh and moved in with us, says John. This is the <u>living</u> word. Jesus still says to us today, "Those who have ears to hear, let them hear." (Mt. 11:15) As we hear, the living word can engage our lives – startling, confronting, delighting, comforting. Does hearing this word stir us to turn to someone and ask eagerly, "Did you hear that? There...there it is again!"

Grace and Peace,
Pastor Shirley

                      Encounter, March 1992
"Heart to Hart" from the Pastor...
    The sun was shining so brightly on the snowy fields that my eyes began to water from the reflection as I turned the car northward onto US 31. I was thinking, however, about a story my father had told me about a picnic and dill pickles.
    The little boy pulled his necktie loose. It usually hung like a rope around his neck anyway by the end of the school days and although all the boys wore them as part of their school uniform and although all of them complained regularly (especially on hot, May afternoons!), this little boy wasn't thinking about the bothersome tie just now. Today he had bigger worries. The school year was nearly over and yet he couldn't think as far as summer days when his only "uniform" would be short pants. First things came first and, for him, that meant the school picnic.

Every year the teachers organized a menu so each child could bring one item to be made into a picnic meal for the whole school. This year, when the food assignments were handed out, the little boy was asked to bring dill pickles. "Dill pickles," he muttered over and over as he scuffed along the sidewalk, kicking at stone, and finding it to kick again. How could he explain dill pickles to Ma? You see, his mother was a Dutch immigrant who spoke English with some difficulty. Would she know what dill pickles were? Would she send the wrong thing? Would he be embarrassed?

The story is about understanding and acceptance, of course, and surely that's why it came to mind because nothing else about my day or circumstances would have jogged it loose in my memory as I headed north on this wintry afternoon. I was visiting a member who had not been able to attend church services here since I arrived last November. In fact, I wasn't completely sure that she would understand that her new pastor was a woman. Explaining a woman pastor is at least as difficult as describing dill pickles to someone who has

> Hart Congregational
> United Church of Christ
> **Rev. Shirley M. Heeg**
> Pastor, Teacher
> 408 State Street
> Hart, MI 49420
> Office Phone
> (616) 873-2449

never heard of such a thing! I was carrying a business card that read, "Rev. Shirley Heeg, Pastor/Teacher," but deep inside I knew that it takes more than credentials to be someone's pastor. It takes understanding and acceptance. The little boy was caught between someone who quite likely (and very honestly) could not understand and others who would not accept a different contribution without ridiculing him. So he pulled nervously at the rope around his neck and kicked at the stone which seemed to be continually in his way. And I knew just how he felt.

When I arrived at the address on my notepad, I rang the bell and introduced myself to the woman who answered. She smiled, invited me in, and reached out, I assumed, to take my coat, but, instead, she gave me a hug. We talked of many things that afternoon, of faith and life, but I didn't for a moment have to explain "dill pickles" to her.

It is so good to work and live with people who accept one another! When I talked with the search committee last summer, I told them quite frankly that I found it difficult to believe I could be warmly accepted as a woman pastor here because such acceptance is so rare! Last week at the Executive council meeting Denny reminded me of that concern. It hasn't disappeared. Memories and insecurities have a surprising grip on us. Yet, I thank God for your genuine openness toward me and my ministry among you.

The best part is that I'm not the lone recipient of such care! Accepting others as they are is clearly part of who you are as a congregation. The Sunday School welcomes children who may only be able to come every other week-end because they are staying with one of their divorced parents. There are no prerequisites for attending worship here. You don't have to know the songs from memory or be a Bible whiz. In these and so many other ways people of this church are quick to open their hearts but slow to point their fingers or throw stones. When we accept differences, and sincerely try to understand, we share Christ clearly and faithfully with everyone we meet, especially those who still struggle with whatever hangs around their neck or looms in their path.

Grace and Peace,
Pastor Shirley

P.S. The "dill pickles" incident turned out fine in the end, too, to the little boy's great relief. Perhaps that's the best part of being accepted and understood – it's such a relief and you feel so grateful to God.

Encounter, April 1992
"Heart to Hart" from the Pastor...

"Wait for me!" "You forgot your lunch!" "No, I didn't. I'm taking hot lunch." "Come on -- I hear the bus! I'm leaving." "No, wait for me! I can't find my shoes!" "We're going to be late." "Here they are. Just slip them on. You can tie them on the bus." "Bye, Mom. Love you."

Each hooks an arm around my neck to pull me down close for a kiss, slings a back-pack onto one shoulder, and off they race, out the door, down the driveway, hoping to beat the bus to its stop.

There's a special kind of quiet that fills a house left behind by a busy, noisy family. The echo of the screen door banging blends with the rumbling arrival of a slowing school bus and then the sounds of shifting gears lift and diminish into the shushing whisper of winds in the treetops.

Although in a moment, the clock will chime again, the refrigerator will run automatically, and the T.V. can be clicked on to fill the room with voices, I know the "quiet" will remain. Although I can fill the house with sounds, I can't replace my "soundmakers."

I remember sharing an impression like this with a friend here at church late one evening after a meeting. We stood in the doorway to the darkened sanctuary and I told her about hollow-sounding classrooms without young people, and eerie gymnasiums after cheering crowds had left. "But here tonight," I added, puzzling, "this place just doesn't seem empty." My friend replied in her own still, small voice, "That's because it's not."

It's not. Not empty. I knew at once she was right. God's presence fills. I'd heard Jesus' words, "Lo, I am with you always." and sung, "He walks with me and talks with me" here in this very room. That's real to me. Yet, just as real are those brief moments, as my family leaves, when I touch on what it means to "feel" alone. Those moments are also significant. Life will bring them around again, more profoundly.

Waiting up for a teenage daughter or son who is out with friends past curfew, sitting in a hospital waiting room looking at bright magazine pictures yet unable to concentrate, coming with flowers to the casket of a sister brother, parent or friend, it's then in a most basic way that we grapple with that stark word, alone. In that struggle, we begin to experience what beforehand we've only read and sung and said about His presence.

Standing in the doorway of the deepest silences of life, we may sometimes still marvel that "it doesn't seem empty here." Even as Christians, there are times when we need to remind one another, "It's not. God is with us."

And at the same time, I can't help but be haunted by the world's empty places -- an aloneness that doesn't recognize His presence. I wonder if our own "absence" times help us hear the fears of others whom our Lord also yearns to draw close. I wonder if those times could nudge us to speak to them.

Grace and Peace,
Pastor Shirley

Encounter, May 1992

"Heart to Hart" from the Pastor…

"Picture in your mind," the storyteller begins, "a towing cliff, thousands of feet high. On the rugged edge, overlooking vast stretches of thin blue sky, perches an eagle. Have you ever seen an eagle get ready to fly? It takes a position, poised on the very edges of the rock, and waits. Why does it wait, this powerful and awesome creature? The eagle waits for the right air currents to come, currents which will provide lift beneath its outstretched wings. A hummingbird beats its little wings so many, many times just to remain in one spot, but an eagle has the ability to spread those wings and glide effortlessly, soaring above storms in seemingly endless skies." I can imagine it happening as it was being described.

In the bible, we are told that we too "shall mount up with wings as eagles" (Isaiah 40:31). Similarly, it seems, we are often readied, only to have to wait on the edges for a while. Surely the breath of God's Spirit will lift us at just the right moment. Just as I am beginning to feel secure and comfortable, the next question surprises me. "But when the wind is right and it's time to fly, what does the eagle have to do?" The room is quiet as we watch the lift-off with our mind's eye. "The eagle has to leap off the cliff and trust the air current to catch it. For a moment it might seem as though it were falling."

While I'm all for restful soaring with the Spirit's support, taking the initial leap of faith is an entirely different matter. My palms are sweaty. I'm reminded how fearful I am of heights and looking down at those rocky caverns below makes me dizzy.

Also maybe surprisingly, this story brings to mind two friends in Christ. One, who was facing major surgery, recently told me she was claiming Isaiah 40:31 for encouragement and strength, "those who hope in the LORD will renew their strength. They will soar on wings like eagles."

The other told me that someone she loved was dangerously close to death, but she had been very moved and comforted when she heard a gospel song on the radio about the way God carries us through.

I thought about how both of these women were waiting upon the Lord. For each of them, no doubt, there were moments when they felt like they were free-falling. As I write this, I know how real and frightening these times have been for them, but I also hear how grateful they are for the peace of God. It's such a joy to see them begin to feel their wings and be lifted above these storms. Perhaps, after all, we are meant to show each other how to leap for the wind.

Grace and Peace,
Pastor Shirley

Encounter, June 1992
"Heart to Hart" from the Pastor...

Please read this! In place of my usual "Heart to Hart" article here, I've decided to ask Adamarie to type the sermon I preached this past Sunday. I want to do this because, as I think of you today, I know there is no message to give you that is dearer to my heart than the message of this sermon. Please prayerfully consider what it says.

Grace and Peace,
Pastor Shirley

The Original Gifted and Talented Program
1 Corinthians 12:4-30

Three weeks ago, I told you that, for the next few weeks, I would be intentionally describing what I saw as the basic elements necessary for this church to articulate its identity and formulate a direction for its future ministry. I have been doing that, without specifically pointing it out each week. Partially that was because of services dedicated to Mother's Day and Children's Sunday, and partially because I am always very aware that, first and foremost, this service is dedicated to the worship of our God and is not a forum for planning or administration. Yet, during this time I've talked with you about caring for others in response to Jesus' call to Peter to "feed my sheep" and about not thinking too highly of ourselves to serve others just as Jesus served the disciples' needs.

From these, I hope you've caught that whatever our direction, it will include an expectation of out-goingness. That **the life Jesus calls us to is an active, attentive, self-giving life.** In fact, I would go as far as to say that if we remain inactive, unmoved, and unresponsive to those around us, it is doubtful if we are Christians at all.

So, if we accept that Christians are to attend to others' needs and serve them – whether "them" means the person in the pew next to us on Sundays or the neighbor down the block – that would seem to lead logically to the next step: to recognize and describe what these needs are and to program ways to meet them. That is exactly what many church-growth leaders advise. It's one path to follow, one that has been followed by other churches in this community and other communities with much success. Here's how it works: if, for example, our community has several young mothers who would appreciate a morning to get together and spend time with other moms while their kids are cared for and supervised, then the church provides such a morning hour. If there are a number of persons who are overweight and who want a support group to encourage their dieting, the church provides a program like Weigh and Pray or Overeaters Anonymous. If teens have no place to gather and talk after ball games, the church manages a coffee house. Some of these ideas are exciting; but if you're like me, you soon come to **these two questions: there's so much to do, so many needs, where do we start? And who's going to do all these things?**

Add to these the fact that we all desire the church to grow and attract new families and youth while maintaining a full and faithful ministry to our current church family and the task seems overwhelming.

Let's survey the territory one more time. God calls us to be active, responsive people. If we are attentive, we will be able to identify some real needs in this community. As a church we can then plan ways to meet and serve people who have these needs, thus, finding opportunities to both demonstrate and tell others about the love of God. It's a marketing technique, you know. Find what the public needs and produce it. Using this product to get our foot in the door, we can also possibly "sell" them on Jesus. As a marketing technique, it is effective. It is also very close to what Jesus did, meeting people at their point of need and demonstrating who he was instead of just explaining. We can find sound Scriptural arguments for this approach, but…is it for us?

Is it for us? What alternative do we have you might ask? First of all, we should look at alternatives if they do exist because we still have our two questions: **With so many needs, where do we start? And who will lead all these programs?**

I want to suggest this morning that we have an alternative in the Scripture before us and that is a preferable one for this church. Let's take a look at the passage together. Particularly, let's look at verses 4-7 of 1 Corinthians 12.

"Now there are varieties of gifts, but the same Spirit; and there are varieties of services, but the same Lord' and there are varieties of activities, but it is the same God who activates all of them in everyone. To each is given the manifestation of the Spirit for the common good." (NRSV)

Varieties, varieties, varieties…Paul is using this word repeatedly for emphasis. The experience of the people of Corinth is that they are different from one another. In our society and time, we might pass over this lightly, thinking it goes without saying. After all, we prize our individualism. We note with pride that each child in a family is unique even though they are raised together. We expect pluralistic views on politics in any group we join as well as different ethnic backgrounds, different values, different personalities, and experiences. But Paul isn't bringing these areas of life to mind here. Paul is talking about matters of the Spirit. Spiritually, he says, we are also very different from one another! Varieties of gifts, varieties of services, and varieties of activities or working – these are all matters of the Spirit. Therefore, when it comes to getting along with one another here or working together, we are not just bringing different backgrounds and preferences, we are also bringing differences in spiritual gifts!

Varieties, varieties, varieties...says Paul but then to each of these he links this word, "same, same, same." Although we may come in as many varieties as savory sauces or as the flavors of ice cream, our God is that same, same, same. There is one Lord, says Paul, who is the source of all this spiritual variety. Just as God is the source of all the other beautiful variety in our world, I might add. Our diverse gifts come from one God; therefore, we accept our variety as many different expressions of one face, or many different instruments playing one composition. We don't struggle against one another, rather we celebrate and complement.

And we use our gifts for the common good, says Paul. <u>We</u> use them, <u>we</u> are active, but it is <u>God</u> working in and through us. <u>God working.</u> That's perhaps the central and most engaging phrase in the vision I'd like to propose. The alternative to the Marketing approach, which hinges on our recognizing needs and filling them, is **a Shared Ministry approach which hinges on our willingness to believe that God will meet needs when we faithfully use the gifts given to us.** We, then, do not have, first and foremost, to be market analysts to assess the needs of our community; we don't even have to address all the needs of our community. God can meet needs through our neighbors, the Methodists, the Baptists, the Wesleyans, and others. We merely need to discover with joy what gifts God has seen fit to give to us, and gratefully put these into use.

How does this address our questions? First, where? Each of us has a gift to use somewhere. So the answer to the question "where" depends on the gifts that show up. On who we are. Not all gifts are equally impressive, but each makes a significant contribution. The hitch is to be confident in that truth. Again, we trust God's provision. We have all the administrators we need to pay our bills and make wise decisions, we have all the greeters we need to extend hospitality to newcomers, we have all the teachers for Sunday School and VBS, we have enough homes with open doors and welcome mats to make friends of those who are new. We do, and we will. I am absolutely certain that we will be serving God in this community in ways that I can't begin to imagine if we follow this vision of ministry because it means that doubt or caution based on human analysis won't deter us. We will trust that God provides where God leads.

Now our questions become: Have you asked God what gift you have? Are you too modest or timid to use the gift that others see in you? Or do you think the good old way is the only safe or right way around here? As a church, we need to recommit ourselves to celebrating the variety of gifts God has given us and to be open to their new expressions as God directs.

The other day my daughter rode into the yard excitedly on her bike. She couldn't wait to tell me that she and her dad had found a new trail. "You go up the regular path a ways and then come to a Y," she said, breathlessly. "Then you go down that way we haven't gone. It's really fun!" Robert Frost, one of my favorite poets, put it this way, "Two roads diverged into a wood and I, I took the one less traveled by, and that has made all the difference." Shared ministry is a bit like that. It's a road less traveled by churches in our market-oriented society. But I think it can make all the difference for us. And what we discover along this path just might be "really fun!"   SH

Encounter, July 1992
"Heart to Hart" from the Pastor…On Pace and Peace

I'm pacing around the kitchen, looking for someone to talk with. God, who am I looking for?

I'm munching one graham cracker after another, starting a new one only to notice a half-eaten square lying on the counter. God, what am I hungry for, really?

I'm finished. Wrapped it all up about ten minutes ago, now what? I like my life to overlap a bit at the seams, God. Why this gap? Why the delay before another beginning?

Do you hear me, God? …God?

It's just like the time one of my young children and I crossed the grocery store parking lot together. Since she was only three or so, I was explaining and giving directions. When I stopped to ask if she understood, there was silence. When I peeked around the bags of groceries in either arm to locate her, I found she'd stopped along the way to upright a ladybug tipped over on the asphalt.

Maybe we'd finish together if I would walk at your pace, God, a pace more childlike. And if I would notice what you notice and take time to stoop where you stoop along the way.

Grace and Peace,
Pastor Shirley

Encounter, August 1992
"Heart to Hart" from the Pastor…

I don't know how obvious it's been to others, but lately, I've been having increasing trouble focusing when reading or re-focusing when I lift my eyes from the page and then return to reading again a moment later. I'm becoming far-sighted with age. For someone who has been near-sighted all her life, this is a strange turn of events. The optometrist prepared me for this change with optimism! He said I'd find that my vision would correct itself to a degree, that my lenses would now be less strong than they have been. But I have to go to see him to have these new lenses fitted and I just haven't found the time. So meanwhile I struggle to focus, to pull together the long and the short of things into a clear picture.

Don't we all? When a child is born, when we hold a grandchild for the first time, don't our minds shift from counting ten perfect fingers and toes to what college he or she will attend with honors? Maybe we should give newborns a regulation football or basketball as a baby gift alongside Mother Goose Nursery Rhymes. In the church we do something like that: we baptize our children saying who they are now, members of the family of God, and we also express our hope that they will pick up this gift at some time when they are older and make it their own.

In August of every year, the committees and boards here plan for the annual meeting by writing reports and reviewing budgets. In a very real sense, they face the same problem: how to focus on the immediate in a way that connects with more long-range goals. Our vision for the future shapes our actions and expenditures today.

Or at least it should. In my years of counseling and working with people, I'm often surprised at how determined we are to manage without adjusting our lenses. We procrastinate. We deny that we have a vision problem. We make ourselves comfortable by either focusing exclusively on the present or on the future, but we adamantly avoid struggling with "how to get there from here." Yet, when we dream for a child, we know that the dreams won't come true if we merely sit and tickle those little toes. We have to teach them how to walk. We have to walk alongside them, to lend a hand. We can't just give directions from the sidelines.

That's why I'm so grateful for the newly formed Pastoral Advisory Committee, for the people who volunteered and who will struggle with the task of evaluating where we are, naming our common vision, and mapping out some routes we might choose to travel together in the coming years. Please pray for us. Talk with us. Let's take a look at things together, for "where there is no vision, the people perish." (Proverbs 29:18)

Grace and Peace,
Pastor Shirley

Encounter, September 1992
"Heart to Hart" from the Pastor…

As the summer draws to a close, I find I appreciate the days differently than I did last June. Do you know what I mean? In June I'm more careless about sunshine and afternoons at the beach. I take fresh bouquets of flowers for granted, right alongside walking around barefoot outdoors or not having to put on a jacket.

But in August, I stop to think about such things. I think about how I value them, how long the winter seems, and how little time remains to enjoy such simple summer pleasures!

It isn't that I haven't always valued summer's warmth and opportunities. I have. I love the summer. But, I use it badly when I think it'll always be around. Some of us are like that about summer days.
And perhaps also about God?

Grace and Peace,
Pastor Shirley

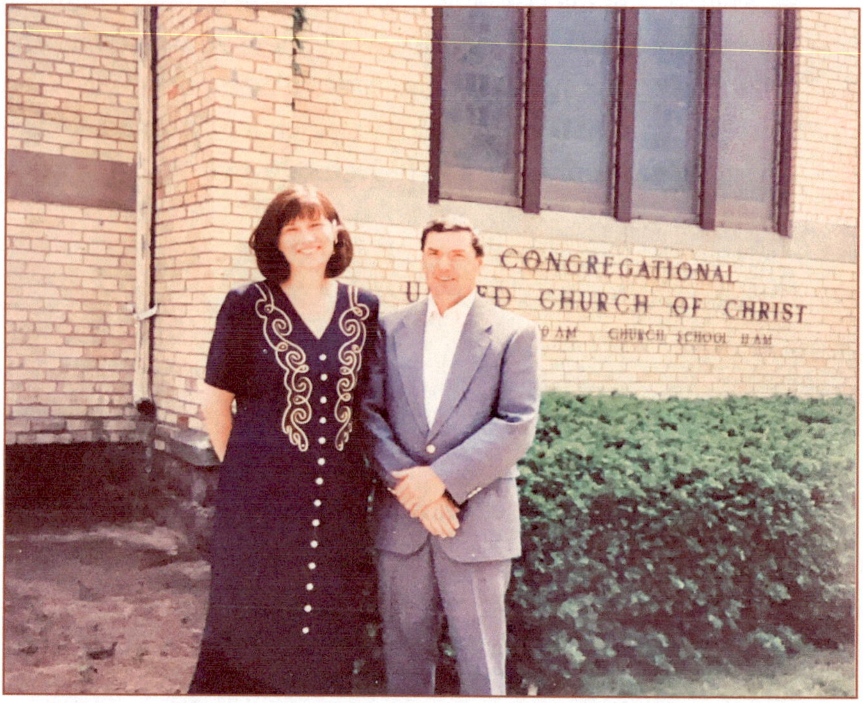
CONGREGATIONAL
CHURCH OF CHRIST

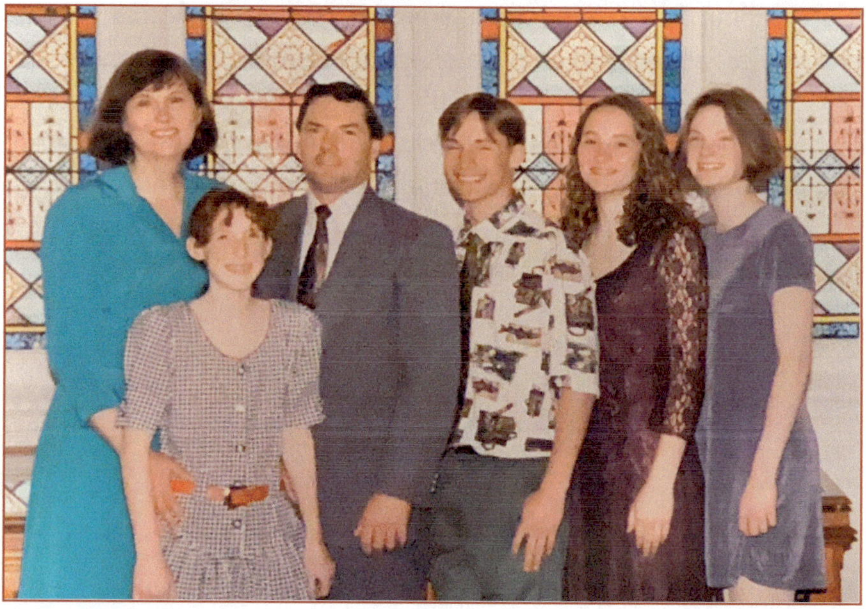

Pastor's Annual Report: October 1992

    Where to begin? This has not only been ten months of learning new names and faces, but also, and more importantly, learning something of the personalities, abilities, and concerns of the people of this congregation. I've been in many of your homes, stood at the side of some hospital beds, planned numbers of events in board meetings, studied with you, prayed with you, sung with you, laughed with you, and felt my eyes fill with tears for your sake. Along with John and our children, I've felt personally welcomed here and I thank you for that. In addition, I especially value the way you have been open to me professionally as a woman in ministry. I thank God for you.

    During this year the church has continued to present an active Sunday School program for our young people, an opportunity for women to serve in Women's Fellowship, the joy of singing in the Chancel choir, and many opportunities to gather around the table together at potlucks, brunches, and coffee hours. Added to these already strong aspects of our life together were a Teen-Overnight-Retreat at the end of the school year, new teen voices in the choir, a Tuesday Sack Lunch and Bible Study, and a Spring Banquet with homegrown talent.

    Worship, perhaps, has seen the most changes. We have included a special time for children during the service, brought the table forward for communion, sung many new songs from the hymnal, and, at times, read modern litanies and dialogues in place of more traditional responsive readings.

    Getting to know you and being involved in these activities and changes has brought some insights along the way. First of all, we need to value worship more deeply as the center of our experience as Christians. Only in worship do we come together as a whole group; all other times we are divided into smaller parts by responsibilities or interests. Only in worship do we focus so fully on our Lord, who is the reason we exist at all. We need to recommit ourselves to attend worship regularly.

Secondly, we need to share the ministry of the church more fully. In previous years you have expressed a desire to be an active people who both minister to one another's needs and to the needs of this broader community. We need to begin in earnest. That's why I'm so enthusiastic about the creation of the Pastoral Advisory Committee and their role in making shared ministry a reality here.

Thirdly, we need to think beyond ourselves. We need to give our faith and our funds away with glad and generous hearts. We need to be an inviting people as well as an inviting place.

In the new year ahead we will pick up many tasks already begun. Once again the church takes up the project of making our sanctuary and fellowship hall accessible by elevator rather than only by stairway. Once again we address how the children can more fully become a part of our worship experience and fellowship. Once again we turn to one another for prayerful care and support.

But even these worthy tasks will be hollow and unsatisfying if we do not see that the church is both our coming and our becoming together. We come to value others when we admit that God loves them as much as God loves us. We become who God would have us be when we allow ourselves to be shaped by God's Word and when we are open to see new and refreshing ways it challenges our lives. Then we have something of real value to offer those who join us.

Grace and Peace,
Pastor Shirley

[November 1992 missing]

Encounter, December 1992
"Heart to Hart" from the Pastor...

I was driving home from a funeral service the other day and as I turned onto the freeway, I reached over as usual to turn on the radio. Immediately an announcer's highly charged voice in an advertisement side-swiped me like a strong wind. It wasn't a new commercial or an unfamiliar station. No, the impact came from the contrasts in my day. Death and a funeral with a mourning family and friends had just collided with life-as-usual in the fast lane. The impact made me stop and think: if both are part of life as we know it, how do people of faith shift from one such experience to the other? And that's when I decided that being a Christian is like standing on one leg.

I'm not accustomed to standing on one leg. When I was a girl, my mother always prodded me to stand up straight, to distribute my weight evenly on both legs. "It's a matter of good posture," she'd say. Otherwise, I'd appear to be leaning to one side. I took her sensible advice.

So it's no wonder I never really took to pink flamingos. They stand on one leg so obviously; they don't even rest the other one on the ground for appearance's sake. But I live in two worlds. To stand on my own two feet is important to me. Or, it is?

With one foot I stand in the church. I stand for God's great, good news that my life is made whole by God's doing. I stand for caring relationships with others as a result of this. I stand in thankful worship. And I stand in hope at the graveside.

On the other foot, I stand as a community member. I stand in lines at check-out counters, I stand up to be counted in the voting booth, I stand in the back for pictures and I grin. I work with school committees, I read magazines and watch TV, I cook and clean, I talk on the phone. On this leg of my life's journey, I take care of myself and of my family and friends.

So - two legs - two worlds, it only seems reasonable to distribute your weight equally.

Yet, at the graveside, I've learned a different truth. At the graveside, everyone stands on one leg or not at all. None of our appointments, none of our hard work, nothing of our helpfulness matters there because none of it offers any hope beyond today's flurry of activity. Truth at the graveside means we will find out what leg we've been favoring. Some people collapse when the death of a loved one knocks their busy life out from under them. But the ones who have been leaning primarily on their faith all along – these stand like serene flamingos, supported and at rest.

We live in two worlds, but the soundest advice I can give you as your pastor is to shift your weight toward faith. Lean heavily on your Lord. It's terrific posture for a Christian and it will stand you in good stead forever!

Grace and Peace,
Pastor Shirley

Encounter, January 1993
"Heart to Hart" from the Pastor...

I love mailboxes. I've collected seven of them to hang on the wall in the entrance to our home -- six for the six of us and one for outgoing mail! It's a great way to sort mail and leave reminders for each other, but I didn't decide to save mailboxes to be better organized. I did it because I have always looked forward to mail.

When we first moved to the countryside, we had to request and wait for a change in the mail route before our mail could be delivered. Those days felt terribly long. I had just left a position teaching school where I had jostled my way through halls crowded with over 400 teens each day. Now I was alone in the woods.

Later that winter when we did have our rural box in place, I remember hearing the distinctive sound of the mail carrier rattling down our snowy-gravel road, then stopping at our box before going on. I eagerly pulled on boots, mittens, coat, and scarf and trudged through knee-deep drifts out to the mailbox. But one day before I could get to the box, the road grader came by and buried it in heavy clumps of slung snow and slush. Although the banks were already way over the box, we had managed to keep the front clear. Now, however, the whole mailbox was buried! I remember scraping the bank with soggy mittens searching spot after spot without success, unwilling to admit I wasn't able to locate it. Finally, with cold feet, tired, and feeling very, very alone, I returned to the house without my mail.

Today I get my mail regularly. I get lots of impersonal mail addressed to Resident or Occupant, but I also get cards and letters that I savor and enjoy again and again. A note means someone has been thinking of me, that someone cares.

We are all called to care personally for those around us, for those God has put in our lives. Yet after a season of card-sending and gatherings, we're tempted to take a "breather" from writing and calling, aren't we? I wonder if we would be more apt to "keep up the good work" if we could identify with those who feel isolated and alone. Mail, of course, is only one way of expressing our Christian love. But it is such a valued one.

I want to share some of my mail with you. Recently I received a note from Betty W.. She writes, "I know for one that you have accomplished one of your goals. You said you hoped to impress the people to express their caring more. They have been wonderful with sending cards and notes. Some days a card in the mail has been the best medicine, so give them a good pat on the back and a big "Thank you" from me."

What Betty describes so eloquently I've heard in lots of different ways from as many different people. Whenever I visit, your caring precedes me in the form of cards and visits. The Women's Fellowship and Diaconate have been beautiful caretakers. And so many of you have responded individually as well. So receive Betty's "pat on the back" and my "keep up the good work!" You are caring people, and your caring in the name of Jesus shines like a light in the winter darkness and warms the soul against winter's storms.

Grace and Peace,
Pastor Shirley

Encounter, February 1993
"Heart to Hart" from the Pastor…

February, the middle of winter, is the month of hearts and sweethearts. I'm glad that February has arrived, aren't you? If you've been attending worship these past few weeks here at Hart Congregational UCC, you're aware that we've been getting back to basics as we study the Apostles' Creed phrase by phrase. I couldn't help but think, at this time of year, how the Creed is for our hearts as well as our heads. And that brought to mind my own attempt to write what I believe. This is called a personal Credo and I wrote it as I was moving from seminary into ministry. I've shared it with various groups including the Classis of the Reformed Church, with which I remain connected, as well as with our UCC Church and Ministry Committee. Now I'd like to share it also with you so that you might know what is closest to my heart in this month for revealing hearts.

MY CREDO

Sitting down to write my credo tonight, I find my thoughts do not first gravitate toward explanations, for I'm very aware that in writing this I'll be doing more than articulating a theology; I will be describing someone I love very deeply. Where do I begin to describe someone I love so — someone I've known all my life and yet about whom I'm constantly learning, someone who has been with me through struggles, anger, joy, fear, pain, and peace and yet has never been at my bidding? As I habitually do with life's questions, I bring them to God. These talks are as natural to me as breathing and just as essential. And perhaps this is where my theology begins; simply phrased, we are not alone. The wonder of Christianity (beyond this beginning which we share with many others) is the revelation that God is not only glorious and powerful but also a God whom we need neither dread nor fear. God is for us. This truth is Paul's underlying assumption in Romans 8:31, "If God is for us, who is against us?" It's not a conditional statement; God's position is certain. We are not alone; God is for us.

I see this statement as a "wonder" precisely because I also hold another basic belief, that God is righteous and cannot abide unrighteousness and at the same time, no part of our being is untainted by sin. This is my condition: I know it to be true of my life. This is our condition: I hear the consequences of self-serving choices everywhere around me, throughout the world, and in the voices of Scripture. Sin screams, laughs licentiously, bites sarcastically, or like an acid, seeps and corrodes subtly and incessantly. Sin destroys. I believe that evil is powerful and that I cannot loose myself from its grip. In sin, we are all over-against God.

Here is where Scripture is critical. While I could know sin from my life and the world as well as Scripture, Scripture alone reveals the seriousness of sin and God's righteous judgment against it. Over and over I hear God calling people to repent and return in true devotion. Over and over I hear God's pronouncement of judgment and I marvel with Jeremiah, Jonah, and others that alongside these pronouncements God waits, suspends judgment, and offers mercy upon mercy.

God's mercy overwhelms God's judgment, it seems. God is for us when we cannot be for God. After the flood God says "the inclination of the human heart is evil" (Gen. 8:21) and yet simultaneously promises not to destroy the earth and its creatures again because of that evil. Reconciliation has been God's purpose from the start. People live in hope throughout the Old Testament, awaiting the "offspring" who would "strike the head" of the serpent (Gen. 3:15) and restore their relationship with God. Paul writes, "While we were enemies, we were reconciled to God through the death of his Son" (Romans 5:10). In Jesus Christ the good news is that we are no longer estranged from God (and therefore also, from ourselves, each other, and the earth). In life and death, Jesus has overcome evil. Salvation comes through righteousness, not a soft-headed tolerance for evil on God's part. And it is God's initiation, God's action toward us, for us, undeserved by us. This is grace.

      The fullest, clearest expression of this grace is the incarnation. This is where I find devotion and description are difficult to distinguish. I can explain something of Jesus' victory over Satan, Jesus' deity, his humanity, and his unity with the Father and the Spirit. However, I'm torn between wanting to make that intelligible to others, yet being most strongly impressed myself by the paradoxes of the gospel story, the aspects that are hard to hold together in my mind, but which have a strong attraction in my heart. I ponder that Jesus "who was in the form of God...emptied himself, taking the form of a servant" (Phil. 2:6-7), that "rarely will anyone die for a righteous person," but "Christ died for the ungodly" (Romans 5:6-7), that in Jesus justice and love coincide, as do dying and conquering death. In the death and resurrection of Jesus, I not only begin to understand how redemption was accomplished, but I also come to know the depth of God's passion toward us. I know this in the way the Hebrews used the term "know"--in an experiential way, through discovery, insight, and intimacy. I know this by faith and at the same time I know that the very faith which receives this revelation is itself a gift from God.

      When I speak of Jesus, I not only speak of my savior but also my Lord and friend. In Jesus' life, I glimpse both the person of God and what human life was meant to be. Although I never can take it all in, Jesus' way with people, his parables and teachings intrigue me. I ask how can a kingdom of God be like a mustard seed or leaven? How can one gain life by losing it? I ask these questions in the midst of my life, as I choose whether or not I have time to visit the woman down the street who has cancer. I ask them as I vote and car-pool, as I watch my daughter wave goodbye. I ask them as I read the newspaper or hear an ambulance, as I re-cycle or attend a town meeting. I ask God in an ongoing dialogue. Here I encounter the Spirit. The Spirit draws things together, makes them clearer, ministers to me and through me, corrects and focuses my ways.

I live in the Spirit. But I do not live there alone. To be in Christ is to be joined to a community of faith, to be joined in God's redemptive purpose for others and subsequently for the earth, for these are linked. To live in the Spirit is to be continually changing. I think one of my most cherished insights is that God comes to us from the future, draws us, and re-creates us in the light of that future as well as the revelation of the past. Therefore, the present I experience is not a distinct segment of time, disconnected from the past (whether my own personal past or the history of humanity and God) or unaffected by what will surely come, the reign of God in its fullness. Time is not as impersonal as we might think. Jesus came into time to be known within time and he has impacted human history throughout time, from beginning to end. Because this is true, I am assured that I can trust God, that Jesus will come again. I find God's assurance regularly comes to us in this way; because God is faithful, when we remember what God has done and has promised, we can live in present dilemmas with hope.

One of my favorite "nicknames" in Scripture is "beloved." I am astonished to be God's beloved in Christ. I can't quite get over it and I never hope to do so. Instead, I only desire to be faithful and true to the one who loves me and to share with others what has been revealed to me.

Rev. Shirley Heeg

Encounter, March 1993

"Heart to Hart" from the Pastor…

Recently a friend sent me a "memo." Now, you need to know that my friends and I don't usually communicate through anything more formal than a hand-scribbled note on the backside of an old bill envelope and, then, seldom do we write in a straight line because we need to conform to whatever shape the edge took when we originally tore it open. So receiving a bonafide, typed "memo" immediately caught my attention. The note had been typed on my friend's computer and quickly brought me up to date on some work we had talked about earlier, but at the bottom of the page she had printed a picture of a haggard woman leaning with both elbows on a stack of papers and books, glasses askew, jaw-dropping. It was a cartoon caricature of herself and I thought it was funny. On our office bulletin board here at the church we have a similar cartoon depicting someone attempting to respond to a dozen demands at once. The telephone keeps jangling, the piles keep piling, and a visitor keeps talking oblivious to all the other confusion. The message is the same: the "busy" part of business can leave any one of us frazzled.

Getting it done, fitting everything in, picking everything (and everyone) up, providing every opportunity for our kids, taking advantage of every bargain, remembering everyone's birthday—whether on the job or around the house, whether the "it" is income taxes or grocery shopping, whether our age is thirty-eight or eighty-three – we keep busy.

The cartoons are funny, but in real life, I know this is where I can get pretty defensive. I love to work. Maybe that's because I love the work I'm doing. In any case, I don't respond well to the suggestion that I'm not only giving work my best but that it might also sometimes get the best of me in other ways as well. I wonder, where is that line between what we give and what the world demands and tries to take from us each day? Can we see it in our own lives or do we just see it in others? I think I smiled at my friend's "frazzled" cartoon because it wasn't my face she had drawn, but her own. Yet, do I recognize the same lines in the face before me in the mirror? Would I admit it to anyone if I did?

Would I admit it to God? That's the bill-board-sized question that greets each of us on the first leg of our journey toward Easter, the part of our trip that takes us through the land of Lent. For Lent offers both a time and a place to retreat from our busyness and to look at the effects of our daily choices, to assess their outcome in the larger scheme of things. Lent is modeled after our Lord Jesus' own time in the wilderness where he struggled with the purpose of his life, what advantages to capitalize on, and which things to avoid. And it reflects, too, forty years of wandering Israelite footsteps on the desert sand, a time and a place when God's people gradually discovered the meaning of reliance and trust.

Memo: Do you ever wonder – perhaps when you're tired or when you've finished one task only to find five or six more waiting for you – do you ever sigh and wonder if you've really got life figured out as well as you think you do? Come, turn aside for a while. Picture yourself here, quietly, thinking things through with God.

Grace and Peace,
Pastor Shirley

Encounter, April 1993
"Heart to Hart" from the Pastor…
In the category of "funniest-home-video-we-could-have-made-but-didn't" comes the following actual dinner conversation from our house:
"You could have passed the potatoes first."
"No, I couldn't…."
"C'mon, we fight about everything."

"No, we don't."

"Yes, we do."

Then in one marvelous moment, everyone around the table simultaneously caught on to the fact that we had begun to argue about whether or not we argue. Suddenly we all began to laugh!

Seeing ourselves – sometimes it doesn't strike us as being very funny, does it? To be perfectly honest, I usually get "touchy" in such instances. Laughing is a less common response. When I thought about what made it possible for us to laugh that evening, it occurred to me that perhaps we can laugh at ourselves when we somehow recognize that we're all in this together. We all participate in the same absurd debates. We're all alike.

On the contrary, we get "touchy" when we feel we're being singled out to be criticized, don't we? And, ironically, by being "touchy" we separate ourselves even further. People approach us with caution, if at all. I guess that's how it works. But, at least it does work, after all; I mean, at least we avoid conflicts that way, don't we?

Yet, after being surprised into laughter the other night, I've begun to wonder if we don't also lose something precious when we choose to withdraw and become "touchy". Realizing we are all guilty stops us from judging each other and also from worrying about how we're being judged, I think. Then we're ready for God's grace! And the instant we're ready, grace bubbles right through because God's been ready all along.

We often talk about "grace" at church, about God's free gift of new life in Jesus, given out of a deep love for us. But how does that translate into our everyday experience? Do we recognize it? For me, one evening recently, it sounded for a moment like the laughter of children.

Grace and Peace,
Pastor Shirley

Encounter, May 1993

"Heart to Hart" from the Pastor...

As I sit here this evening in the quiet of my home, I can hear the muffled cough of one of my children as she sleeps. Now and then the dog curled at my feet will sigh and shift her weight into another position. And somewhere a long way from here, in another rural community, the embers of a fire snap and collapse as it slowly burns itself out. Horrible fire. The apocalypse predicted by and, very likely, also arranged by David Koresh, a self-styled Messiah.

In our conversations here through the months, I have often been informed by your analysis of world events and your acute perception. That's why I have no doubt that many of you have already begun to reflect on the meaning of this event as well. Sifting thoroughly through facts and reasons, we seek to understand why.

Why? In the coming days, psychologists will venture views as will reporters, congressional leaders, FBI spokespersons, and victims' relatives. By the time you read this perhaps more information will be available. Or perhaps other news will have already dulled the edge of this event and the question will be packed away as it so often is, unanswered.

But tonight as I sit here in silence, I remember the words of an early church leader, Augustine. He wrote, "O God, our souls are restless until they find their rest in Thee." And I wonder how often restless souls are the answer to "why?"

Restless souls kindled by incendiary claims, caught up in wisps of hope, not knowing how to discern between truth and lies -- I ache tonight for those restless souls who sought their rest in David Koresh and settled for death rather than life in Jesus. How were they to know? A bit of Paul's letter to the Romans echoes this concern: "But how are they to call on the one in whom they have not believed? And how are they to believe in one of whom they have never heard? And how are they to hear without someone to proclaim him?" (Romans 10:14)

Paul is talking about being sent to share God's good news. I think Paul's sense of urgency comes from his ability to see everyone he meets as a "restless soul." And I pray that God will give us that ability too. We need to share our faith, people. We need to tell our children what God means to us. We need to invite our neighbors to Sunday School – yes, the adults. And sit with them, listen to their experience of restlessness, remember our own, and share the truth we have come to know. We can't sit back and wait.

Deeply grateful for how God's grace and peace surround us.
Pastor Shirley

Encounter, June 1993

"Heart to Hart" from the Pastor…

The other day in the grocery store while I was waiting in line to check out, I couldn't help but overhear the conversation between the woman ahead of me and the cashier who was bagging her purchases in one of those new plastic bags with the loop handles. I have to admit that I was mildly surprised to hear the customer say, "You'd bag all my groceries in those bags if it were up to me. I really like them. They're so easy to take out of the car and carry into the house." The cashier, however, only partially agreed. "They're no good for bread items, though, because they don't stand up," she replied as she put a bag of hot dog buns into a more familiar brown paper bag alongside the others.

Well, I didn't give that much further thought then, but this morning I'm wondering again. I wonder how many of us – and especially, I guess, how many of us together – accept changes positively and incorporate them into our lives. I have some ideas about that. Change just to be different is hard to justify, although I do like variety from routine. Change is difficult because it always brings with it some measure of loss – loss of familiarity, of security, of predictability, and so on.

Who opposed the first automobiles? What about the blacksmith union? And I remember the depression in my own neighborhood as a child when the railroad laid off firemen long after their primary function, stoking the fires to produce a good head of steam, was obsolete. Some changes are wrenching because they alter our lives irreversibly. And changes like these leave us no choice. They are forced upon us. They produce tremendous stress.

So why change at all if change brings all this discomfort with it? To improve? Because we are stuck in a place that isn't good for us and others around us? Because staying the same is an illusion; we are either moving forward or going backward? Yes, and because God calls us to change. To "become" the children of

God that we are. Paul writes, "And we all, with unveiled face, beholding the glory of the Lord, are being changed into his likeness from one degree of glory to another; for this comes from the Lord who is in the Spirit" (2 Corinthians 3:18). Simply put, the Spirit is committed to changing us.

And I wonder, are we any more open to this sort of change than to other changes in our lives? Are we willing to let God pack what we need into new shapes for our future?

Grace and Peace,
Pastor Shirley

Encounter, July 1993
"Heart to Hart" from the Pastor…

Someone telephones. I can hear one side of the conversation only as I sit in the next room at my desk. An emergency. Through a scanner, someone has heard that an ambulance has been sent to the home of a member who has been ill. In the background, I hear the soothing sounds of a classical music selection on my radio and the birds are chirping as they cheerfully build a nest in the dogwood just south of the church.

Here in front of me scattered across my desk like prematurely fallen leaves are yellow pages from a legal pad with notes about our anniversary celebration in August, the Jr. High mystery trip, the program for this week's potluck, an outline of Saturday's wedding ceremony, and some background notes for my sermon. It's Tuesday morning and I've already visited two hospitals this week.

Laughter, fears, hopes, doubts, work, rest, sorrow, struggles, wonder – life is certainly full!

Here at the church we are planning more events and activities as a congregation these days and there's a spirit of anticipation growing among us, isn't there? I'm excited about the events ahead, but on mornings like this, I'm also profoundly touched by the depth of our ministry together, by the willingness with which we, who are naturally rather independent sort of people, are now daily sharing our burdens and joys with one another.

So as I reach for my car keys to follow the ambulance this morning, I'm thankful to God who is always with us in every experience. I'm thankful for hopes and delights, for comfort and strength. And I'm thankful to belong to a people of ever-deepening faith and service.

Let's continue by God's Grace and in God's Peace.
Pastor Shirley

Encounter, August 1993
"Heart to Hart" from the Pastor…

I remember Grandma wearing lots of purple. Her hair was the whitest of white and, although she meticulously pinned it in place with white Bobbi pins that I would buy for her at Woolworth's, nevertheless on warm summer afternoons like these, a few ringlets would invariably stray out and soften her already beautifully gentle face just a bit more.

That's how I remember Grandma, dressed in a crispy purple frock with a sparkling purple brooch and with a lively face encircled by hair that was at the same time as bright as light and as soft as dew. That's how I picture her whenever she comes to mind. You see, Grandma died a few years ago. But she still comes to mind often. I think of her, for instance, whenever I drive past a field with purple vetch vines curling every which way. And in my nostalgia, I might even happen to think how she might have enjoyed discovering it with me if she were here today.

Yet, as my mind trails off to follow such lovely thoughts, I'm stopped abruptly. I'm stopped because I can still hear my

Grandma as plain as day grouching about the very plants that now bring her to mind.

"That vetch is such a nuisance," she'd say. "Tangles your feet when you try to walk through it. Ruins the hay. Can't even cut a decent length strip for a bouquet that will stand up properly in a vase."

My Grandma was invariably practical. My memories have the luxury of not having to be practical at all. Memories can wag this way and that, they can take on a softer-than-real glow, they can color one impression more vividly than another.

I couldn't help but think of that as our church family nears our 125th Anniversary Celebration. I think we've all been looking forward to looking back. And I've been as delighted as a child to discover the stories that we share as our common heritage. Yet, I want more than anything for us to hear the real voices of those who lived through the difficulties and hopes of these 125 years. I don't want us to glorify those who went before us, because they don't glorify themselves.

I laugh aloud when I read some of the accounts in our archives. Like the time the congregation met in a dance hall before our building was built. There had been a dance the night before and the same musician who played at the dance was now playing for the worship service. He made it clear, though, that he was using a different fiddle, one he kept just for worship!

Then a little girl came in, just as the service was starting, and tried to walk across that highly polished dance floor to her seat with snowy balls still stuck to her shoes. She slipped and fell unceremoniously on her bottom. The pastor, trying to maintain the decorum of worship in spite of this event, turned rather sternly to the choir and asked them to sing something quickly. So the choir sang "How Firm a Foundation." (Evidently, a sense of humor has always been a qualification for joining the choir here!)

Out of such real people, God formed this church. Through the years they argued as well as agreed, mourned perhaps more than they rejoiced, cried with one another as openly as they laughed at themselves. But through the years, woven in and out of every account, lacing so many stories together, has been the consistent theme that God is building this church, that God hears and answers often in surprising ways, that no difficulty is too difficult for God. Therefore, again and again this church has been a people who have been able to face challenging and frustrating realities without despair.

Anniversaries tempt us with nostalgia, yet, it's my hope that our 125th will remind us who we really are, once entangled in sin, now set free by grace, and that we will glorify God alone!

Grace and Peace,
Pastor Shirley

Encounter, September 1993
"Heart to Hart" from the Pastor…

I was looking at the face in the photo and I was stunned to realize that it was almost me – a young girl whose mouth seemed to grow into her grin while, at the same time, her eyes were shrinking. But although those features were so very familiar, they were only almost-me. For they were, in fact, my mother's. I was looking through an old photo album my sister had brought over. I could just as easily find her high cheekbones and slender frame draped in a filmy gauze dress of the 1930s. (It was probably a 1920s carryover since those times were so hard!) Of course, it wasn't her at all; it was my grandmother. Perhaps the most wonderful and often quite astounding discoveries in family albums are family resemblances. When looking back, we can expect to find our ancestors, our roots, and our heritage, but now and then, perhaps unsuspectingly, we turn a page and are startled to find ourselves, aren't we?

That's my most recent (and frankly somewhat surprising) discovery here at the church as well. Returning once again to the stories and photos of our early years, I have found that I'm recognizing us! And I think such realizations are only drawn when we take a second or perhaps even a third or fourth look.

It's there in heated discussions and reluctance to embrace change when congregational churches were asked to consider banding together as the United Church of Christ – that independent glint of light in the eyes. Or it's there in row upon row of robed children singing sincerely in pageants for their parents – the emphasis on Sunday School that caused a congregation to put its Board of Christian Education on an equal footing with the Diaconate and Trustees. It's there in the warm smiles around tables of food – lasting friendships that run deep and true.

We value what they valued before us. It's our family resemblance. But I can't help but also look further back into the past, to a time before photos, before newspaper clippings, to picture the stories of God's people throughout 2000 years of church history. Here are people of hope in hardship, people of persistence through persecution because they are people who trust their savior and friend, Jesus our Lord.

It's also true, you know, of the people of Scripture whose faces we will surely recognize as our own, if and when we take a closer look. These are our stories, our struggles, our amazements, our frustrations, and our fears. But most importantly of all, this is our God, in and amidst, over-shadowing and enlightening every picture, every face, and life.

The church has long been and still is a place to meet God personally, a place to learn what is really of value, a place to find yourself. I wonder, how often do you find yourself here?

Grace and Peace,
Pastor Shirley

Encounter, October 1993
"Heart to Hart" from the Pastor…

October again. Ahhh! How I welcome the fresh October air into my lungs! October's harvest colors soothe the deep recesses of my eyes. I find myself walking the wooded hillsides, ducking under low-hanging limbs, stopping to gaze in amazement as the sunlight sifts through layers of branches in a way that is just simply glorious as if it has been patiently waiting for me and this moment to come together at last. I've always felt at home in autumn.

At times I come across phrases or words that affect me like that as well. I mentioned in a recent sermon that I particularly like to hear the invitation, "Come, sit with me." I'm also touched when someone says, "I'm glad you're here. I've missed you."

And I especially like the way some people say "thank you" so that you know right away that they really mean it. (Denny P.

has that wonderful way about him. I've often appreciated that and it came to mind once again as he presided at our annual meeting this past month.) How I welcome words that are genuine and unassuming amidst the everyday traffic of hurry-up, high-pressure demands! But I sometimes think that few of us ever get our fill of what truly refreshes our spirits.

There are places like that and words like that – where you can be yourself and feel that you belong.

That's the way prayer can be.

The way deep Christian friendships can be.

And the way a church can be when we walk together and discover the glorious light of God's love.

"Come to me, all who labor and are heavy laden, and I will give you rest. Take my yoke upon you and learn from me; for I am gentle and lowly in heart, and you will find rest for your souls." (Mt. 11:28-29)

Ahh, yes!

Grace and Peace,
Pastor Shirley

Encounter, November 1993
"Heart to Hart" from the Pastor...

He sat in the car, long after he'd turned off the engine - just sat there, in his driveway. He knew how it would be if he went inside the house. They would be surprised to see him. They would make a fuss. And the air would be stuffy, both with noise and supper smells. There would, no doubt, be questions as someone set another place at the table and one of the children ran to fetch the extra chair from the spare room. He would be worried about where he would have to sit and, thus, distracted, perhaps he wouldn't hear their questions well enough to answer. No, that's not entirely true. He knew the questions already beforehand. Even alone here, in the dark car, they came to mind. "Where have you been so long?" "What made you finally decide to come home?"

Or maybe no one would ask after all. Maybe they would be silently polite, not wanting to tip the balance lest he slip away from them once again. Would that be better? Or, would such silence be more deafening, more stifling than the noise?
Would he have a place inside? What if they didn't recognize him at all? Or, what if they didn't want him?
Light streamed through the house windows. Above, slanted rays almost reached the cold metal surrounding him. It was probably warmer inside there too. Brighter, warmer. If the truth be known, that's what drew him this close now and again. But he just couldn't bring himself to get out of the car and go in. It was too overwhelming.
As he shrugged, started the engine, and began to back away into the night, he thought, half wistfully, "Funny, how after all these times, no one has come out to notice me here."

Our Lord Jesus concluded one of his parables with these words: "And the master said to the servant, 'Go out to the highways and hedges and compel people to come in, that my house may be filled." (Luke 14:23)

Go out.

Grace and Peace,
Pastor Shirley

Encounter, December 1993

"Heart to Hart" from the Pastor…

And so it begins, another Christmas season. "What a wonderful time of year for you!" a friend reminded me the other day. Immediately so many wonderful memories came to mind – the garland hung just right in the front of the church, golden flames reflecting in the eyes of acolytes as they light the Advent candles, Christmas-red cheeks, and the sound of carols sung from a hay wagon. So much happens here at Christmas time.

Alongside these, of course, are all our personal traditions: family gatherings, company parties, school vacation, shopping, putting up the tree, programs, and concerts. These contrast with appeals for help, wars, and poverty which seem all the more tragic and cruel, don't they? Hype and glitz cheapen even such a beautiful time, along with short tempers, too-high expectations, financial stress, and loneliness. So it begins. Or perhaps, in this instance, continues, but at a heightened level.

I wonder how it will be for you this season – wearing or wonderful? Or some of both? I suspect the events will come off well; the cameras will click and flash to save our smiles. But will our relationships deepen? Our love grow? Will we be even more deeply moved by God's great compassion for us?

And so the season begins. And while much is familiar and perhaps reassuring, nothing is absolutely predictable, of course. Jesus came into familiar surroundings in the lives of the people of Bethlehem too. No doubt families gathered for reunions during this time of tax collection and some were working 2nd and 3rd shifts with their flocks or at the innkeeper's desk. But the birth of this child drew them all aside and filled them with hope and wonder. It happened then and, in these days, it begins again.

Grace and Peace,
Pastor Shirley

Encounter, January 1994

"Heart to Hart" from the Pastor...

How to begin? In my own life, I face that question, perhaps, more often than any other question. It comes to mind as I look at this empty page before me now just the way it does each time I sit down to write a meditation or newsletter article or sermon for you. It comes to mind each time I'm determined to call on someone I barely know. It surfaces after each plunge I take into "hot water" in my relationships when conversations can seem so awkward: How to begin?

And it's an appropriate question as January returns, isn't it? 1993 was our 125th Anniversary year and a wonderful anniversary it was! Christmas carols are still ringing in our ears reminding us of the birth of our Savior. But it doesn't end there. It doesn't end with memories of the heritage we share, or with crowds singing "Silent Night"; it begins there. One thing I'm sure of: We cannot begin by closing the books and going our separate ways for the long, dark winter days ahead. We were not created to hibernate. We were created to love and to express that love, first to God and then to others and ourselves.

How to begin? Open the books. Hear the stories we each carry inside ourselves. Gather to hear the Scriptures read, taught, and proclaimed.

How to begin? There's only one way to fail: not to begin. Our God continually invites us into new beginnings!

Grace and Peace,
Pastor Shirley

Encounter, February 1994

"Heart to Hart" from the Pastor...

Schoolchildren know it. The school year actually begins in September. But they also know that the year begins <u>again</u> in late January. This second beginning, the second semester, is a second chance.

For many of us this is a time of renewed efforts, isn't it? Some enroll in aerobics to get back into shape; some take computer courses to adapt to these new information-at-our-fingertips times, (just ask Tom Stevens!) We organize last year's receipts and do our taxes to clear that obligation out of the way. Whether it's learning, health, or finances – in mid-winter, we buckle down, dig in, and get at it once again, don't we? We tend to take care of our minds, our bodies, our families, and our businesses with renewed attention and energy these days.

And there's a vigor that comes with "second semester". But isn't it also time to add your inner self to that list of things that need attention and renewal? What refreshes your soul?

I just talked with someone who is thinking of joining the chancel choir. Hurray! What a gift to yourself, both to enjoy this group of people and also to take a beautiful melody (or harmony) along with you all the rest of the week!

This month some will join the church, taking a new step in their faith, exercising it in new ways. Some will be baptized, entering the church's sacrament of death and rebirth with Christ through God's grace. We're singing a new song as we leave worship each week, a song that names ways we can live what we believe wherever we go. We're starting a new Sunday School semester for adults as well as children: new attendance records, new books!

So, what are you doing to attend to the needs of your inner self? That's an important question to ask. You see, the church doesn't send out reminder cards for "6-month check-ups" or automatically make appointments for you with our Lord. Yet, as God's people, we can claim with Paul, "We do not lose heart. Though our outer nature is wasting away, our inner nature is being renewed every day." (2 Cor. 4:16)

Every day. This is what God intends for us. Have you taken advantage of this offer? Perhaps this is the time to begin again!

Grace and Peace,
Pastor Shirley Heeg

[March 1994 missing]

Encounter, April 1994
"Heart to Hart" from the Pastor...

During the season of Lent, the church encourages each of us to take more time for devotions and our own spiritual growth. But it would be a mistake to interpret that expectation solely as an individual concern. I'm impressed continually with how the Holy Spirit moves when we commit ourselves to both personal and corporate expressions of faith. Listen to what I've heard during these past few weeks of Lent:

"Pastor, we need to pray more in small groups together. How can we do that?"

"Do we ever have confirmation classes here at the church? We need one. How about this summer?"

"There's a wonderful mystery to our faith, isn't there? Beyond all our understanding, we stand in awe of God, don't we?"

"Pastor, I've had someone come to me with a particular problem and I don't know how to help. Can you talk with me about how to be a caregiver in this situation?"

"It isn't enough to invite people to join us in worship and

be friendly. We have to know how to connect more. We really have to connect with God and each other."

I can't remember when so many significant concerns have arisen among us during such a short period of time! Surely, God is stirring us. Surely, it's time to be about these things. So, I'm planning a summer session for inquirers who would like to learn more about our beliefs. Please let me know if this is for you.

The adult Sunday School class continues to gather after coffee time around a table in Fellowship Hall each Sunday morning for a lively discussion on the book of Hebrews!

Some thoughts about prayer groups are beginning to come together as well. What do you think? And so on, and so on…

We are different from one another; we have different needs. Our understandings and choices differ. Yet, our diversity can bring delight to any of these opportunities to come together. Diversity is refreshing!

And unity recognizes that there is something deeper that we share, that bonds us and gives our lives their true meaning. We are one in Christ.

The seeds of Lent have been faithfully planted. Let's see what grows in the months ahead!

Grace and Peace,
Pastor Shirley

Encounter, May 1994
"Heart to Hart" from the Pastor…
Whatever happened to humming?

My grandmother used to hum while bustling around her kitchen waiting for the tea kettle to boil, I recall. But somehow it doesn't seem to be the thing to do while waiting for the microwave to beep when your coffee's hot. How long has it been since you found yourself humming? Or, came across someone else humming? Whatever happened to humming anyway?

I miss humming, now that I think of it. I wonder if that's because I miss what humming comes from, what it means. There's a peaceful unassuming quality to humming. (Lyrics draw attention to themselves and tend to call others to listen and think along.) Humming doesn't strain anyone, neither the hummer nor the neighbor happening by. And humming's hopeful-sounding in a "new morning" sort of way, isn't it?

Now I love all sorts of music. (I'd buy a car for the sound of the stereo, not the engine!) I love the excitement of live concerts. I love singing God's praises with you here at the church. But it strikes me that humming is what lingers after the stereo's shut off, after the crowd disperses. Humming shows how deeply the song sank into you. Humming is responding.

Living the Christian faith is supposed to be like that, you know, the constant hopeful humming of your soul.

Grace and Peace,
Pastor Shirley

Encounter, June 1994
"Heart to Hart" from the Pastor…

Sometimes life is so wonder-filled that I'm awed just to think of it! And even as I write that sentence, I know that for so many among our church family, the days are lined with times to take medication and hope that stiffness or congestion eases by noon so you can move around better. One part of me says, "How can you be so cheery in the presence of such real suffering? Isn't that insensitive?" But another part of me – the wiser part, I'm coming to believe – has listened long enough and deeply enough to those of you who struggle with life's difficulties each day to have learned something about your outlook. It's an outlook drenched in God's grace and goodness even in the midst of everything you have suffered and it's an attitude that, in itself, is something I find to be one of life's wonders.

And so, alongside you, perhaps especially honoring those of you for whom life is more difficult now, I welcome the summer. I breathe deeply of lilac-scented breezes and let the smell of newly turned soil stop me in my tracks for a moment. I like patting the three-legged dog that haunts my neighborhood gas station and miss her if she's lounging in the shade somewhere. I love the many shades of green that God uses. I've discovered that even forest-green pine branches have paler, spring-green tips these days.

And the sound of two robins quarreling over my backyard as if it were their own territory makes me smile. But so, too, does the booming radio driving down State Street toward me encased in a teenager's car with windows wide open. The taste of fresh asparagus purchased from a roadside stand or a crisp radish from John's vegetable garden are also some of the delights of my days. (I think I only love radishes now because they have the good sense not to ripen at the same time as sweet corn which out-distances them for taste by a country mile!)

I know each of you could make a list like mine. A list of wonders, of the delights of life that surround us every day – the environment in which we work and make decisions and get things done. How about just listing these in your next prayer? Being thankful. It's another of life's wonders how a simple thing like thankfulness can liven your spirit and lighten any burden.

"Bless the Lord, O my soul! O Lord my God, thou art very great…the earth is satisfied with the fruit of thy work" (Psalm 104:1, 13B)

Grace and Peace,
Pastor Shirley

Encounter, July 1994

"Heart to Hart" from the Pastor...

Do you know who won the lottery? Well, it wasn't exactly a lottery... His name was Matthias and as he was chosen, another fellow (who had 3 different names) blended back into the congregation of a little over a hundred other nameless followers of Christ. (The event is described in Acts 1:15-26). When I think about Joseph (or Barsabbas or Justus), I wonder how he accepted the decision. Was he honored even to have been nominated (as the Academy Award losers claim each year?) Was he disappointed or hurt? Did he feel as if God had rejected his gifts and abilities or at least preferred someone else's service to his?

And I wonder about Matthias sometimes. To be chosen by God for the express purpose of apostolic ministry must have been exciting, but a little scary. Peter had said they needed someone to fill a vacancy, "to become a witness with us of His (Jesus') resurrection." (vs. 22) But the 11 had been through so much together. "Remember when Jesus...," one might begin and others could eagerly join in the conversation, retracing their steps, and reliving shared experiences. I wonder how they included him while reminiscing.

And how did they support him in ministry? Could he make a suggestion without being discounted because he hadn't been with them very long? Did they accept him, encourage him, bring him up to date, this Johnny-come-lately named Matthias?

And the crowd. Did they relate to this new apostle with the same love and respect they had given the others, those who had been their leaders from the beginning? What would it be like to replace Judas Iscariot? Would some approach him with skepticism, at best hesitancy? Would others, with great insight, who had always known there was something strange about that Judas guy, seek him out as a champion for their position?

I don't know. Acts 1 tells us only "So he was added to the eleven apostles" (v. 26). Evidently, it all went smoothly. The dynamics of working together are often challenging. Occasionally I wonder how they carried it off, but mostly I wonder how we would.

Grace and Peace,
Pastor Shirley

Encounter, August 1994
"Heart to Hart" from the Pastor...

The child grips his grandmother's skirt with one small fist and tugs to signal that he wants to be lifted up. In a moment he whimpers and tugs again because Grandma, who is in conversation with a friend, hasn't seemed to notice. Still listening, she automatically lifts the tired child onto her well-worn hip, a hip that once held his mother.

Let me hear of your steadfast love in the morning, for in you I put my trust. Teach me the way I should go for to you I lift up my soul. (Psalm 143:8)

The young woman lifts item after item from her grocery cart and places each one on the wide belt to check out.

....to you

The hay is baled and now, as I watch, strong arms are lifting heavy bale after bale and hoisting them onto the wagon.

...I lift up.

I look up and stare at nothing really. I'm engrossed, perplexed because I can't see my way through the problem in my mind. I'm afraid there may not be an answer. Or, maybe, I'm afraid of what the answer may be.

....my soul.

To be a Christian is to go through the motions daily. To lift up my soul to the one who loves and guides me. To do it as surely and as naturally as I move the muscles of my arms. No matter whether my soul is heavy, or tired, or matter-of-fact, or even collapsed in upon itself. I lift it up to the One I trust.

Grace and Peace,
Pastor Shirley

[September 1994 missing]

Encounter, October 1994
"Heart to Hart" from the Pastor…

Sometimes I wonder what your thoughts are. Coming out of the experience of teaching school, I feel more "in touch" when I'm actually with folks so we can enjoy the give and take of conversation. Writing can feel pretty one-sided at times, but it doesn't have to be.

When I read the letters that the apostles wrote to the early churches, I hear them talk about nearly everything with their readers – including how to wear their hair (it's in there!), who to eat with, as well as attitudes towards work, and personal troubles.

And I've noticed that the apostles often call their readers by name, listing those who have been especially helpful recently right alongside those who need to make some changes in their lives. (Writing to the Philippians, Paul even calls out some women who have been arguing and tells them to stop it!)

But, I wonder as I study, just how in touch we are. I wonder if we really want to be known that well after all – not only by each other, but more importantly, by God. Wouldn't we sometimes almost rather NOT hear a personal message from God?

Sometimes people tell me that they don't get answers to their prayers and that they can't hear God. I don't always know what they expect, but I DO know that God has already spoken. The Bible we hold in our hands is God's word. And the church teaches that this is the LIVING word. I think that means that we will find these words are "in touch" with each of our lives – that whenever we come to listen, God will talk with us, perhaps in comforting ways and yet, also perhaps in a discomforting way.

That's the chance we take when we choose to listen, isn't it? Maybe that's why we sometimes choose to avoid it instead. As a people, we pray readily, but have our prayers become one-sided conversations? How long has it been since any of us prayed, "God, sometimes I wonder what your thoughts are. So today I'm here to read your word and listen."?

Grace and Peace,
Pastor Shirley

Hart Congregational Church to dedicate new elevator

The Congregational United Church of Christ of Hart will dedicate its new elevator during worship Sunday, Dec. 11 at 10 a.m. The elevator provides barrier-free service both up to the sanctuary and down to the Fellowship Hall. Those who need such assistance or who would find such access a convenience are invited to park their vehicles in the paved lot south of the parish house. The elevator has its own ground-level entrance on State Street on the southwest corner of the church building.

The elevator is the realization of the congregation's long-held hopes to make their church more readily accessible to those who have difficulty with stairs. In August 1993, on behalf of the church, the trustee board accepted a matching-funds donation and set the goal of having all necessary funds in hand to finish the project by the time of construction. Many donations and memorials were designated toward this effort throughout the coming year enabling the congregation to complete the project this fall free from debt. The Congregational United Church of Christ is especially grateful for all who gave so generously.

The community is invited to join the church for this dedication service. ◊

Encounter, November 1994
"Heart to Hart" from the Pastor...

"That's the way I look at it!" The words sound confident, don't they? They may even sound like something of a challenge as if the person speaking is daring the rest of us to think differently. But certainly, even if you or I don't disagree with him this time, someone, somewhere, on some occasion will disagree, isn't that true? We are a people of differing opinions. We may associate with one group because we find we have much in common or we may separate ourselves from others because our opinions clash. (Or, vice versa! Sometimes I think folks deliberately seek me out to express opinions that contrast with my own just to see what will happen!)

That's why I was especially struck by a passage of scripture I read this week. In Matthew 22:23-33, Jesus comes across a group of people who already have their minds made up. They already believe that there is no life after this one. They have decided this because they are particularly careful about obeying the law of God just exactly as Moses has laid it out for them. And since Moses never actually said anything specifically about life after death, they have decided that there is no such thing. Their opinion can be traced to what they believe. Who can find fault with that? Who could ask for more?

Jesus for one. Jesus is asked to comment on a particular situation that the Sadducees describe, and he gives them a thoughtful answer, but I was most impressed by his first few words. In verse 29 Jesus says, "You are wrong, because you know neither the scriptures nor the power of God."

Opinions need to be revised. They need to be freshened. They need to be remodeled. As one of my dear friends once explained, "Some people may think of me as a stick-in-the-mud, but I continually remind them that it's only mud. It's not cement." Have our opinions about life and death, about God and faith, about what gives life its meaning and purpose – have these hardened like cement? Jesus reminds us that we have more to learn, not only more by returning to the scriptures, but also by watching what God is doing. God does what is more right than any of us can imagine and in ways that we would never think of. (So, how confident are we about those old answers we hold?)

Jesus, our Lord, didn't condemn the Sadducees for the limited opinions they held, but he didn't leave them there either. He taught those who would listen and verse 33 tells us that "when the crowd heard it, they were astounded at his teaching."

Grace and Peace, (and Astonishment too!)
Pastor Shirley

Encounter, December 1994

"Heart to Hart" from the Pastor…

"She wrapped him in cloths…" (Luke 2:7) And so, the greatest gift was wrapped late on that first Christmas Eve.

How good of God to come to us in the Christ child! Wrapped in the body of a child, God is not nearly as frightening as we might otherwise expect.

Of course, this gift was not at all what the people of that small, captive nation expected. They wanted a much bigger gift, one with more power. They wanted, once and for all, to be able to call their neighbors out into the street and shout. "Aha! Look what we've got!"

What do you do when you get a baby for Christmas? You learn what love is all about.

And, quite possibly, you learn what love is NOT about. Not leverage to use against someone else, for example. Not decoration to make yourself look good, powerful, or important.

Tonight the winter winds are whistling around the house. As I reach for the afghan, I think what comfort is expressed in the simple act of wrapping! And what better comfort is there than to be wrapped in God's love!

This holiday, may you again know the real warmth of Christmas. And may you be quick to enfold others who still suffer in this cold world.

John and I, along with our children, Elyse, Anne, Aaron, and Merileigh want to take this opportunity to send you our personal Christmas greetings. God's blessings to each of you. We love you all in the Lord and look forward to sharing with you whatever God brings in the year ahead.

Grace and Peace,
Pastor Shirley

Encounter, January 1995
"Heart to Hart" from the Pastor…

"Did it seem like Christmas to you?" the clerk looked up and asked.

I was surprised by her question. I had overheard her conversation with the young couple just ahead of me in the check-out lane, but that had been merely casual, like most conversations at cash registers. This greeting took me off guard. (And for a brief moment, I wondered why she had selected me to hear it.)

But, then, I wondered about how to respond. I sensed she had more to say so I cautiously returned the question to her. No, she said, it really hadn't seemed like Christmas, not for her, and not for many of those who worked with her here at the department store according to her unofficial count. "Perhaps the lack of snow," I lamely offered, thinking of the number of times I'd heard someone on the radio over the past few weeks "dreaming of a white Christmas." I had a terrible headache and just wanted to move on.

"Well, maybe," she conceded without conviction. Then she added, "I've been waiting all morning for a phone call from my daughter. She went into labor again this morning and I had to drive her to the emergency room." By now, she was furiously sliding my purchases across the scanner, finding each bar code with her fingers almost as if it were in Braille.

"That's why I came in late today," she added, looking up with her eyes while keeping her head tilted down as if sharing a confidence. "It's the second time she's gone into labor this week."

The woman paused. She just stopped, suspending a bottle of aspirin in mid-stroke. I looked longingly at the aspirin. But, I knew, too, that she had more to share. And this was the important part, significant enough to break her otherwise impervious working rhythm.

"They won't tell me if she phones," the woman said, in a carefully controlled half-whisper.

"I'll pray for her…and you, would that be ok?" I offered, nearly as quietly.

"Oh, yes, thank you," she brightened, and a familiar beep from the scanner punctuated the remark. She was back in full swing again, handing me my bag and reaching for the next customer's first item on the belt almost before I could manage to take mine in hand.

I don't know if that moment seemed like Christmas to her, but it did to me.

It seemed like God was "among us." The two of us – I with my headache and she with her deep concern to hear about her daughter and new grandchild – stood not in the fluorescent light of that store, but for a moment, stood together in a special way in the light of God's abiding love.

As the new year begins, I urge you to take Christmas with you. There are people everywhere for whom it has not yet arrived. The United Church of Christ says, "To believe is to care, to care is to do." Do share God's love in the new year!

Grace and Peace,
Pastor Shirley

[February 1995 missing]

Encounter, March 1995

"Heart to Hart" from the Pastor...

This morning as I came down the back walk, I shifted my book bag, purse, shoes, keys, and gloves into one hand so I could pull open the back porch door to the parish house just the way I always do. That's when the feeling first hit me and, to tell you the truth, it took me by surprise. After all, I had only been gone for one Sunday. And who gets sentimental at the sight of an old familiar screen door? But there were the dependable bags of salt for the sidewalk that some thoughtful person had set out and, once again, I found myself thinking the same old thoughts as I fumbled to put my key into the lock.

"I'm sure glad that someone thought to surround this porch with walls. Great windbreak. I wonder how many pastors or their wives have been sheltered here from the bitter March wind while they juggled their parcels and reached to unlock the door."

That's what being gone for a Sunday does to me. I miss this place; I miss the folks here, even the "cloud of witnesses" who came before me. And being gone just makes me all the more aware of the everyday things that make me feel happy and thankful. It's good to be home.

The next season of the church calendar is called Lent, a time to think about ourselves, our faith, and the meaning of what God has done for you and me. For many of us, the story is familiar, but each time we return to the heart of it, we realize anew how precious it is, don't we?

Those who have been away from church for a while, who have been getting along without giving faith much thought, may be surprised to find that the simple act of returning holds a deep appeal. Here you can be sheltered from life's harsher blows. And you may discover that even if you have both "arms" full juggling work and school, meetings, and recreation, coming home to Jesus so satisfies your soul that it's well worth the effort.

Lent is a time for unlocking our lives and opening them up once again to the warmth of God's love.

Grace and Peace,
Pastor Shirley

Encounter, April 1995
"Heart to Hart" from the Pastor…

"Worry is not worth the time," I hear a woman remind me, much the same way she's reminded me before. It's one of her principles; in the time I've known her, I have come to believe that she lives by it too which is one of the reasons I listen. But as I drive to another home to visit, I hear another twist on the same story. This woman also believes that worrying is pointless, but doesn't know how to break the habit.

Some days I just wake up happy. I had a lot of those days when I was a child. Then over the years, I remember those times growing fewer and farther between. But I still occasionally wake up some mornings just awfully grateful. "This is the day that the Lord has made. Let us rejoice and be glad in it!" I recite the familiar verse, Psalm 118:24. But God also made yesterday when I was feeling discouraged.

Living the faith is not based on feeling faithful. Feelings, however, are a big part of my experience of life and are in themselves a gift from God. Yet good feelings are so fragile, aren't they? There are so many factors that influence our feelings: health and exercise, responses from others, fatigue, unforeseen difficulties, and temptations.

Where is the balance? Do I discard my feelings and live only based on what I know? I've been betrayed often enough by what I thought to be true to know I should sometimes doubt my knowledge too. What I know doesn't always remain so.

The Bible would put in a good word here for trust. Trust is counting on someone when entering the shadowy regions of doubt. Trust extends its arm out full length to grasp with confidence what cannot be seen in the fog.

"Blessed is the (one) who trusts in the Lord, whose trust is the Lord. (This one) is like a tree planted by the water, that sends out its roots by the stream, and does not fear when heat comes, for its leaves remain green, and is not anxious for the year of drought, for it does not cease to bear fruit." (Jeremiah 17:7-8)

Trusting God even more than you trust yourself. Can you imagine that? Many of us are still trying our faith on for size, seeing if the color looks good on us, perhaps ready to toss it aside again when the weather is pleasant. But trust keeps our lives steady. That's because the One we trust has nicknames like "Rock" or "Steadfast Love."

Trusting in God's Grace and Peace,
Pastor Shirley

[May 1995 missing]

Encounter, June 1995
"Heart to Hart" from the Pastor...

    I've seen it again and again and it still amazes me. Just last night I saw it twice in a matter of a few minutes. I was at a meeting of the Parkinson's Support Group that is just being newly formed here when I noticed it first. Right in the middle of an informative and helpful conversation, while gathering names and organizing future programs, there it was. One of the members had brought a piece of art that he had painstakingly completed. It was obviously the product of an imaginative spirit, much concentration, a keen eye, and deliberate handwork. As he passed this around, he had this message to share, "We've got to keep active, do what we love to do, and use our minds and lives to the fullest!"

    I watched as his craft was passed from hand to hand around the circle of folks who had gathered. I watched their hands at first, but almost immediately their eyes drew my attention. They were eyes that valued the care and hard work that went into creating this piece of art. While I found the piece of art beautiful, these eyes helped me appreciate his accomplishment in a special way.

    Later I joined the choir at their Spring party, walking into the midst of laughter as they gathered around the player piano and sang. The rippling keys, the steady percussion of pumping pedals, melodies and harmonies, swaying and gestures, what a pleasant confusion of folks and fun! And there in the midst, I found it again. When I stopped to fill my plate with goodies from the dessert table, two separate people took me by the arm, leaned toward me, and asked, "Did you see the bird nest?" Sure enough just outside the window tucked under the canopy was a small brown twig nest. When I moved the blind a bit to see closer, the mother bird (so small to be a mother, I thought) fluttered away momentarily. Our noisy enjoyment inside and the beautiful return of spring on the ledge outside were so immediate and at the same time so fragile and transient. How precious!

I marvel that life is so good even amid its aggravations, frustrations, and pain. The church has long named this characteristic of our experience, "common grace," meaning that joys and provision that God pours out for everyone out of that great God-sized love. It's "common" because it's what we have in common. However, sometimes the word "common" can come to mean something that isn't special, that is mundane or ordinary. This week as I marveled anew at the hope and everyday goodness God offers, I was struck again by how truly uncommon and remarkable God's "common" grace is!

But I say to you, Love your enemies and pray for those who persecute you, so that you may be children of your Father in heaven; for he makes his sun rise on the evil and on the good, and sends rain on the righteous and on the unrighteous. (Mt. 5:44-45)

Hmmm….I wonder how uncommon it is for others to discover God's remarkable, amazing "common" love in us.

Grace and Peace,
Pastor Shirley

[The Parkinson's Support Group was organized when four or five members were diagnosed and we discovered there was no such group in the county. It included both those with PD and their spouses or care-givers. Attendance wasn't limited to church goers, but rather open to all who were interested. At one point between 50 and 60 people came. We met at the church monthly for a potluck dinner followed by guest speakers, ranging from the Sheriff to a neurosurgeon. They covered many topics, including how to move more easily, medications, and when to stop driving, etc.. Being together was the real benefit, however. We always had time for caring prayers.]

Parkinson's Educational Program
West Michigan

Located in Grand Rapids

Encounter, July 1995
"Heart to Hart" from the Pastor…

Whenever she opened her mouth these days it seemed she was corrected by someone. At least that's how it felt to her.

When she said she missed the folks at church because she had to work on Sundays, her friend Ruth had said, "But God loves the people you work with too, dear."
When she said she was stressed by so many bills coming in at once, Bob said "You should have planned ahead."
When she said she worried about the kids, Tom said, "Christians shouldn't worry about anything."
When she said she was finally going to speak to the boss about how unfair her workload had been lately, Gina reminded her, "Everything is in God's hands and you should patiently, even joyfully, accept whatever God allows to come your way."
When she said she was tired, they said, "No wonder, you work too hard. Don't you know enough to rest? Get a hobby. Take a vacation."
When she protested, they said, "Well, we sure are touchy today, aren't we?"

When she was a little child, Wednesdays were always prayer meeting days. She guessed that was why she still resorted to praying smack dab in the middle of things, even yet.

"God," she said just checking, "you do know that what I say at any one time is only a part of what I mean, don't you?"
"And God," she asked, "do they really believe they can resolve my concerns in less time than I can take a breath when I've been struggling with them for so long?"

"And God?" she went on with a sigh, "Why do I feel so lonely?" Then before God could get a word in edgewise she jumped in again, "I know, I know, YOU are with me always!"

And God smiled and kept right on listening.

Grace and Peace,
Pastor Shirley

[August 1995 missing]

Encounter, September 1995
"Heart to Hart" from the Pastor…

The child has been watching eagerly at the window for what has seemed a lifetime, but now he jumps backward off the couch and races to the front door. "Grandpa! Grandpa!" he exclaims. "I'm so glad you're here! Now we can make my tree house, can't we, Grandpa? Can't we?" "Yes, today we'll begin to build that tree house," Grandpa responds, cradling the upturned face between the palms of his hands. In that moment of greeting, they look into one another's eyes and rejoice in each other's presence. And together they envision the task ahead.

How will they proceed? Building projects often have complex blueprints. Puzzling over them would be one place to begin. No doubt that would be beyond the boy. The task itself might be beyond Grandpa's physical abilities. Maybe Grandpa could give the boy verbal directions from a distance. Or the boy could be left to follow his own free choices and Grandpa could return later to point out the failures in his unsupervised attempts. Should the boy be entrusted with the project at all? Grandpa could conceivably intervene while the boy is sleeping and complete the project without him. Perhaps the boy should be expected to learn principles of construction and recite them competently before he is ever handed a tool. To the outside observer, there would seem to be much to deliberate.

But not so for these two. When Grandpa extends his gentle, experienced hand, it is grasped by a small dependent one and they walk out to survey the huge, old oak together, talking and sharing confidences. It will be a task done in relationship for neither of them would have it any other way.

A task done in relationship – that's ministry! See how often the Scriptures refer to conversation. Deuteronomy 6:7 calls out to us: "Teach them [the words of God] diligently to your children…talk of them when you sit in your house, and when you walk by the way, and when you lie down, and when you rise." Isaiah rejoices in the gift of "The tongue of those who are taught…to sustain with a word him that is weary" (Isaiah 50:4). The very identifying mark of "God's own people" as they are described in 1 Peter 2:9 is "that you may declare the wonderful deeds of him who called you." Teaching, talking, sustaining, declaring! Are our words and tasks expressive of our relationship with God?

Grace and Peace,
Pastor Shirley

Encounter, October 1995
"Heart to Hart" from the Pastor…

How grateful I have been all year for your continued devotion to God and for your ongoing dedication to the work of the church! And how wonderful now to name the hopeful beginnings that we've seen together because of this commitment:

The beginning of a Parkinson's Support Group, the only one in our county, meeting the needs of several of our own people and reaching out to others who are suffering.

The 11:15 a.m. Contemporary Worship on Sunday mornings (which we sometimes hold outside on the green) features a simple order of praise songs, the presentation of God's Word, and prayer.

The beginning of the OUTREACH Committee's church-wide visitation program in April renewed our relationship with many in our community and invited them back to worship, an invitation that many accepted.

The Pictorial Directory – a kind of "family album" – will help us in the time ahead to recognize each other and keep in touch better, a wonderful beginning for relationships to grow.

The beginning of not only a new curriculum for our Sunday School but also a whole new approach to teaching: a hands-on, experiential method that promises to touch lives in deeper, more lasting ways!

The beginning of a new solvency as we are in much better shape budget-wise this year than last while giving to mission through our United Church of Christ OCWM gifts remains as strong as ever.

So much of what happened here quietly throughout this past year has been healthy and good, but of all these things I am most excited about the new faces around here, about the children in worship as well as in Sunday School, about the coffee hour conversations where we can get-acquainted with each other. I love the faces of those who trust God during times of pain, struggle, or confusion. MOST OF ALL, I LOVE HOW WE'RE TRYING TO LOVE BETTER!

The theme for the year ahead is CHANGE. I believe change, for us, will especially mean expressing kindness to those beyond our normal circle of friends. Change will ask of us a willingness to give up our own comfort, our time, our own way to make even more room for others, to welcome people into the loving arms of the church, to stop complaining about different ways of doing things, to stretch ourselves even further, to take risks or, at the very least, to allow others to take prayerful risks.

Now and then I think it is important to remind ourselves that we serve a God who created a brand new world not only at the beginning of time but also (perhaps to our surprise!) calls to us at the END of our Scriptures, saying, "Behold, I make all things new!" (Revelation 21:5) God is about newness -- new life, new songs, new opportunities. We need to be doing what God is blessing in the new church year ahead!

Grace and Peace,
Pastor Shirley

Encounter, November 1995
"Heart to Hart" from the Pastor...

When November 1st rolls around this year, I will begin my fifth year as your pastor here at Hart Congregational United Church of Christ. In some ways, I'm as amazed to be your pastor today as I was when you called me and we first promised to serve our Lord together! I'm amazed that you would place your confidence in my call to ministry. That you would trust me as you have. I'm amazed how God has blessed us with closeness to one another, with ideas and hopes, with hospitality taking special delight in newcomers, with familiar laughter and song. I'm amazed at God's goodness as I see it expressed again and again in our experience.

I'm amazed and I'm grateful. Last month was proclaimed to be "Pastor Appreciation" month by those who do such proclaiming. I discovered that in a lovely way – gradually, like the blooming of a flower. Now and then, scattered all through these past few weeks, I received the most wonderful messages from you! I have cards piled up on my desk here at church and stuffed onto my windowsill at home. You have held my hand and spoken with me. You've given me hugs. The diaconate chose two beautiful deep-red mum plants for my garden.

Still, life has not been all roses (or mum plants) for us this past month. What a loss it was to hear of Tom S.'s death and once again, to stand with you between our own human sorrow and spiritual rejoicing for him. After September's annual meeting, October brought new members to our boards and committees and new agendas for the year ahead. By now our mushrooming Sunday School has met enough times to give us a sense of how we're doing as teachers and to set us to work getting the bugs out. For me, two services on Sunday mornings means more opportunities for praise and joy, but it also means giving up those great talks we have had during coffee times in the past.

So it's in the midst of changes, in the midst of losses and joys, that we come to this anniversary of our time together. And with a fresh awareness of the power of encouragement in my own life, in this month of nationwide Thanksgiving, I am going to the Executive Council with this request:

> **That together we proclaim
> this our fifth year together to be a year
> in which we intentionally give thanks
> each month for a particular blessing
> and particular persons here among us.**

Each month, then, we will announce the focus for our thanksgiving on the first Sunday and in the *Encounter*. That way, throughout the weeks ahead you can express your thanks both to God in prayer and to others in that gracious, thoughtful way you have.

Surely we have much to be thankful for, much too much to stuff into one day. Thankfulness is such a wonderful therapy for anxiety, too, you know. I think that's one of the reasons Paul recommends it to his parishioners in Philippi who have had their share of suffering as well as joys. Let me close with his words, "Rejoice in the Lord always; again I say, Rejoice…Do not worry about anything, but in everything by prayer and supplication with thanksgiving let your requests be made known to God. And the peace of God which surpasses all understanding, will guard your hearts and your minds in Christ Jesus." (Philippians 4:4, 6-7) May such thanksgiving, such peace be yours!
Pastor Shirley

Encounter, December 1995
"Heart to Hart" from the Pastor…

I went out Christmas shopping last week along with all of you and everyone else on the western side of the state, I think. The stores were busy and lines were long. Nevertheless, I was able to scratch several items off my list and jam it back into the side pocket of my purse before I shifted my bags and began to leave for home. In a hurry, with my arms so full and my purse dangling, I almost ran over a little girl who stopped suddenly right in front of me to look at a display of nativity scenes just at her eye level. She stopped so I stopped. And I couldn't help but look at the figurines too.

Everything was there: shepherds carrying sheep; wisemen, one kneeling, robe flowing in folds, holding out his precious gift; camels; a cow; Mary with her golden halo; Joseph with his arm outstretched as if to point to the manger; and the baby Jesus in the hay. Not bad, I thought, still wearing my "shopper" hat. The facial features were rather carefully done. A lot of detail. I winced, 'though, to notice that someone had set the whole scene up in the wrong "building." In place of an angel and the words "Gloria Deo" across the peak of the roofline, there was another sign. Under a window with diamond-shaped panes, there hung a sign that read "Candy Shop." Evidently, the backdrop for this scene was intended for the Alpine village on the next table.

Just as I was wondering if the set came with a stable or if the pieces were sold separately, I noticed that the little girl was reaching right into the scene. At that same moment, my "shopper" hat was sounding alarms in my ears. "You break it, it's yours!" signs flashed before my mind's eye and I could almost hear stern, cautioning adult voices from my own childhood. She went straight to her task, however, and with soft-mittened hands, she carefully, reverently lifted and cradled baby Jesus, manger and all.

In Luke's account of the event the angels say, "This shall be a sign for you…" or perhaps, as it's translated by Eugene Peterson in his contemporary paraphrase, *The Message:* "This is what you're to look for…".

As I watched the little girl, I finally had the good sense to take off my "shopper" hat and bow my head. You see, I was on "holy ground." With all my judgments about whether the scene was "right" or not. I had forgotten momentarily what God had sent messengers to tell me to look for. And in that moment I saw that even "Candy Shops" have angels. One of them is just about waist high and wears her heart on her mittens. And, although she didn't say a word, she spoke to me as eloquently as those first Christmas angels, "This is what you're to look for…".

"Glory to God in the Highest!
And Peace"…to you.
Pastor Shirley

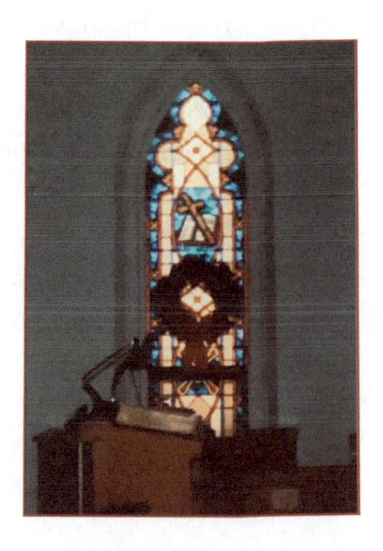

Christmas Letter
December 1995
Dear Friends,

At Christmas, God comes to us in a very personal way to say, "I love you!" And each time we celebrate this holiday, that is the very best way to do it, don't you think? To say "I love you" with our words, in our giving, with a touch, in our laughter, with our listening, in as many ways as there are stars sparkling in the clear winter sky overhead at the close of the day.

It's that kind of love that John and I have known here again this year – love for us and love for our children – patient, kind, thoughtful love that has seen us through time and time again. It's that love that we also have in our hearts for you. We love you and we thank God for you daily!

As I write this tonight, the whole season of Advent stretches ahead of us. When I was a child, I could hardly wait until Christmas, but as the years have passed I have learned to savor things more. Tonight, as your pastor, I'm glad for all the plans we've been making together and I'm looking forward to watching them unfold. I'm especially glad for all the people around here who can't imagine Christmas without lots of ways to give of themselves. (Do you know that every resident of the Medical Care Facility will receive a hand-written Christmas card from us delivered by the upper-elementary Sunday School kids?) This month we will sing carols to those who are shut-in; we will collect food and new, warm hats and mittens to give away; some of us will volunteer with the Good Samaritans to pack and deliver boxes of gifts and food to families in our area. And we will have a lot of fun doing it because, as the choir sang just last week, "It is in giving that we receive." Although a loving life is not without its sacrifices, it also offers deep joys. What an adventure! And all this in a time when others think first of their inconvenience or complain often of being bored!

I'm also looking forward to worshiping our Lord with you. How carefully the sanctuary has been prepared for the celebration of Jesus' coming! How faithfully the choir meets each week to practice and perfect their tone! Families will be lighting candles for us; lay people will be reading and praying on Christmas Eve. I'm excited about studying the nativity story this year with special attention to the messages of the angels. And when we are all ready to begin on Sunday mornings, we will hope to echo God's "I love you" back up to the heavens.

Merry Christmas, from all of us with love!
John, Shirley, Elyse, Anne, Aaron, and Merileigh

Encounter, January 1996
"Heart to Hart" from the Pastor…

Well, we've opened all our presents. The tree is looking sadder and older now that they're no longer clinging to her skirt. While the gifts have moved into our already crowded rooms, the tree, on the other hand, will soon move out. Today we'll take down our sentimental ornaments and store them for another tree. And we'll put Christmas away for another year.

I have never liked putting Christmas away. It's not just frustration with taking things apart, not just the mess of bringing up cardboard boxes and packing tissue from the basement. I miss the lights. I miss the brightness of wrapping paper and candles. I miss the figures I carefully placed out: shepherds, Joseph, several Marys, and baby Jesus; they have become my companions. I wonder, as I have wondered before with living friends, if I have really taken the time to gaze at them long enough to hold them in my memory for lonelier times. I long for the wise men to leave me some wisdom for the year ahead before they depart, but one morning they're just gone like the rest.

I have a head cold. I rummage for some cough syrup in the cabinet. It's back to work, back to school, back to appointments, back to bills, back to normal. People who have been here over the holidays have all returned home. I will not hear again from many who sent me cards until next Christmas. Between now and then, a lifetime will pass. There will be winter storms. There will be nights when I worry about my family. I will get tired. Of course, there will also be Spring, but that seems far off as I tuck the tree-top star into its box.

Putting Christmas away is a modern problem. It isn't a part of the original story, you know. Remember those shepherds whose ordinary work was interrupted that first Christmas? Remember how they rushed to the mangerside? And then they, too, spent time with lots of other folks gathered in town, talking about what they had seen with enthusiasm. They celebrated Jesus' birth. And the story ends with these words, *the shepherds returned.* Did they return to the night shift on the hillside? Did things go back to normal? Did they blend in again with the rest of the crowd and get on with their lives? Yes. *The shepherds returned,* but the story doesn't stop there! In Luke 2:20, we read they *returned, glorifying and praising God for all they had heard and seen, as it had been told them.* Notice this is AFTER they had been out all night telling others. It is AFTER the party! The shepherds didn't box up Christmas and put it away. Even AFTER that first Christmas, their lives were never quite the same again!

Christmas – the way they knew it – had little to do with what was "sentimental" and ornamental" and much to do with relationships. It had much to do with what light represented: love, truth, the reign of justice, clarity of purpose, and, most of all, hope. *Glorifying and praising God* is another way of saying "thank you" for all of that! And saying "thank you" to God became the way they went on, the way they carried the blessings of Christmas into their future.

As you store Christmas away this year, store the best of it in your heart! When we are thankful to Jesus for coming into our lives, the New Year will surely be bright!

Grace and Peace,
Pastor Shirley

Encounter, February 1996
"Heart to Hart" from the Pastor…

In front of me on the desk is a picture of the Big Lake taken a few summers ago. The day was clear and beautifully blue-on-blue, with pale blue sky meeting dark blue water at a steady, unwavering distant horizon. The sand in the foreground is rumpled like a blonde blanket and gray and green poplars poke through the dune here and there. I can see the faces of my family, all grinning. I remember the day. But today is a much different day.

Through my window, I see another shade of clear -- the watery clear color of ice on glass. And here too is a blanket of sorts, a heavy comforter of white covers us all, and feather-light flakes swirl and tilt from side to side as they fall. They're piling up. Often as I write I focus on people and the things we do, but today I just want to take a long look at this blue and white and tan and sometimes green and red-orange earth that so constantly and beautifully surrounds us and supports us.

I know that, for some of us, the dunes are too steep; the sun, blistering hot; and, even in summer, the water can be shockingly cold. In winter we know that black ice is slicker than gray, and sometimes even crusty snow is a blessing if you have to walk. Nothing is warm enough. But if the weather does thaw, we get colds. And cherry trees, their hopes stirred up, are likely to be frostbitten and lose their summer potential. We contend with the earth.

And yet, we also enjoy the earth immensely. We snow ski and water ski. We provide sunflower seeds in winter and hummingbird syrup in summer, inviting birds over for a meal. We dig in the dirt, we transplant and fertilize, we water and cut back in gardens quilted with colors of our own choosing. We cherish the smell of rain, the drama of a storm, the peace of a lake at sunset.

That's how we feel about the earth, in varying ways at varying times. It is always much with us. But when I turn to the Bible also on my desk, I'm mildly surprised at how often I hear NOT how people feel about the earth, but how the earth itself feels! Here during this winter storm and dreaming about summer, I thought it might be good to scatter a few of these verses before us.

"For you shall go out with joy and be led back in peace; the mountains and the hills before you shall all burst into song, and all the trees of the field shall clap their hands. Instead of the thorn shall come up the cypress; instead of the brier shall come up the myrtle; and it shall be to the Lord for a memorial, for an everlasting sign that shall not be cut off." (Isaiah 55:12-13)

"Even the sparrow finds a home and the swallow, a nest for herself, where she may lay her young, at your altars, O Lord of Hosts, my King and my God." (Psalm 84:3)

"For the creation waits with eager longing for the revealing of the children of God; for the creation was subjected to futility, not of its own will but by the will of the one who subjected it, in hope that the creation itself will be set free from its bondage to decay and will obtain the freedom of the glory of the children of God. We know the whole creation has been groaning in labor pains until now; and not only creation, but we ourselves." (Romans 8:19-23)

The joy, the sense of safety and care, the frustration - all these are the experience of the earth as it contends with us and with God. The world is a passionate place, a beautiful place, our place, a gift from our God, to be reclaimed and renewed by our Lord Jesus. How wonderful to take all that in on a snowy winter's day!

Grace and Peace,
Pastor Shirley

Encounter, March 1996
"Heart to Hart" from the Pastor...

Last week my sister called to tell me that our Dad was driving up from Grand Rapids to her home in Montague to fix her lawnmower (yes, lawnmower!) No matter that the schools were closed because of ice, that snow-covered anything that was even remotely green in her yard, no matter that he had to drive on slush-covered roads, he knew her lawn-mower needed to be fixed and he believes that broken things need attention.

Some people say my Dad and I are a lot alike. I'm not sure that always holds true. For example, he knows more about lawnmowers than I ever care to know. But I wonder if I don't borrow his approach when it comes to the church.

There's a common-sense saying that we hear nowadays: "If it isn't broken, don't fix it." In other words, don't pour a lot of time and energy into things that are just fine the way they are. It's an efficient approach to life. Yet, on the other hand, doesn't it make just as much sense to take care of something ASAP if it *is* broken? Broken things need attention. Surely that truth applies to human brokenness as well.

The man held out his right hand so his buddies could see that he was missing the end of his littlest finger. "Lost it a few years back when trying to remove packed, wet grass from a lawnmower blade," he said.

"What do you think I did first?" he asked. "Did I think, 'Oh, that fingertip is just a small part of me, not very important?'

Did I think, 'I can get along without that fingertip? It never made much of a contribution to my life anyway. Not all that good-looking either? Did I fling my arm out wide like this, casting that bleeding finger as far from my heart as possible?

No, I'm telling you the first thing I did was to pull that finger in real close to my chest, to hug it to the center of me and hold it gingerly because it was wounded. I was wounded. Now I ask you, do we do the same when others are?"

That's one of the best questions that I've ever heard. Jesus heals. The effect of prayer on physical healing is widely accepted not only in the church but also in the world today. But the Spirit of our God moves to heal ALL our hurts – including our emotional, mental, and deeply spiritual ones.

We probably agree on that too. But here's the rest. That reaction. Much of human healing happens within a community. We need each other. We need the touch of each other's love and support. We need the balance that thanksgiving brings into our lives. The church needs to hold its wounded very tenderly and draw them close to the heart of God. The church needs to respond despite inconvenience, to go the distance, to weather all sorts of difficulties simply because it is important to attend to what is broken.

If you are hurting, know that you are loved here. Sometimes you may need some space from people, a retreat from crowds. We will respect that decision. But if you have felt forgotten or cast aside when you were hurting, that's our failure and we are sorry.

If you are strong, remember that the love people find most believable is the love that shows up. That's what Jesus was all about -- God saying, "I've come just as I promised."

Grace and Peace,
Pastor Shirley

Encounter, April 1996

"Heart to Hart" from the Pastor…

It was late one Sunday evening. I was sitting on the white couch in the church parlor behind the sanctuary. The table lamps lit the page before me and I thought the arched stained glass window was even more beautiful against the dark night than it is in the morning light when I usually see it. Time for Bible Study. A small group of us have been reading the book of Colossians together throughout the season of Lent. **There in the dark silence, I read these words aloud: "For you have died…"** (Colossians 3:3)

Died? I have died? I thought this was about Jesus' death. Oh, I know that I will die…one day… "If something happens to me," as we say.

"If something happens to me, make sure the good dishes go to my daughter."

"If something happens to me, tell him I loved him so!"

"If something happens to me, be sure to sing 'Wonderful Grace of Jesus' at my funeral."

"If…", we say "if." Most of us haven't even come so far as to say "when" yet, although we know that death will come, don't we? "Two things are certain: death and taxes," we say. And, taxes are due real soon now. Death? We'd like to hold that at arms' length at least, so we say, "If…". Perhaps, in moments of truth, we may venture to say, "when…," but God says to those of us who call Jesus our savior, "You have died."

It makes me think of those who have tombstones carved before their deaths. I remember walking on Cemetery Hill in

Shelby and stopping before one of those joint stones to read the dates of birth and death for a husband, noticing at the same time that the date of death for his wife was still left open. "She must stand here like I do," I thought. "Reading her name on the stone." "You have died…" says God. Furthermore, perhaps what is more astounding – **that's the good news!**

When I make chaplaincy calls in the hospital, I often talk with people who have just come from surgery or new mothers soon after their deliveries. Invariably, they are relieved that these critical moments are behind them and now they are on the other side! But the difference is that they actually had to endure the experience! In our case, God not only awakens us with the good news that it's all over, but we also hear how we have been spared. "For you have died, and your life is hidden with Christ in God."

When all our sin met all of God, the sky darkened, the earth shook, and the holy temple was ripped open! When all of God met all of our sin, a heavy boulder rolled away like a mere pebble, bright angels burst in, and life had the last word, "Aha!"

There was no place I could have found to hide from all of this except he hid me. And now that it's all over it's OK to come out. It's OK to trust and live. "So consider yourselves dead to sin and alive to God in Christ Jesus." Paul writes to another congregation (Romans 6:11).

Consider yourselves dead…and alive! We can't be alive to God and alive to sin at the same time. Even a little bit of God and a little bit of sin is an explosive mixture. If we have died to sin, our lives can no longer be wrapped up in getting ahead, in resentments, in selfishness, in foul talk, in fantasies and flirtations, in power, or greed or gossip and the like. When you and I come out of that tomb where we have been hidden with Jesus, are we ready to leave our grave clothes behind?

Grace and Peace,
Pastor Shirley

Encounter, May 1996

"Heart to Hart" from the Pastor…

As I sit down to write this, it's nearly midnight and April 30th is about the turn into May 1st. April showers bring May flowers I remember. But what do April snow flurries bring? Chest colds and weariness, I'd say, judging from my conversations with many of you.

The winter has been too long.

The winter weather has worn us out. Sometimes I think the winter-like experiences of our personal lives also tend to last way too long and often seem too much to endure. Recovery takes far longer than expected. Marriage troubles don't seem to have any resolution. We just can't seem to break our bad habits no matter how often we begin again and again. At those times, our patience can wear as thin as an old coat against life's bitter winds. Or we can keep on believing…

> I believe
> in
> spring-earth richness,
> soil-smell greenness,
> and deep, dug into
> life.
> I believe
> in
> God with sleeves rolled,
> handling earthness,
> from loved seeds, slowly,
> gently
> lifting blossoms.   SH

Grace and Peace,
Pastor Shirley

Encounter, June 1996

"Heart to Hart" from the Pastor…

We worked hard all day. Spring had finally come almost neck and neck with summer in its heat. No time for the luxury of Spring fever this year, no time to dawdle over the aroma of lilacs along the picket fence or to dream while holding hands on those meandering walks through the emerging garden.

"If we don't get raking and digging, there will BE no garden," I warned. "If we don't scrub winter's grime off the windows, the summer sunshine won't have a chance to brighten the house."

So we worked hard all day. And by supper time, we looked like it and felt like it. "I'll go for a pizza," I said, raking my hair with my fingers and winding the elastic holder around one more time to keep it off my face. One of the kids went along so I wouldn't choose toppings that no one would eat but me. We were tired and hungry and in a hurry. That's why when I saw the sign that read "WE SELL UNBAKED PIZZAS," I immediately decided to get one. That would be quicker than waiting for a pizza to be baked there and maybe I could even shower while it was baking in our oven at home.

The young man took my order, "one large deluxe unbaked pizza." Then without looking up from his pad, he asked, "Will this be for here or to go?" It was a routine question. He asked it every time anyone ordered a pizza, I'm sure. But an UNBAKED pizza for "here"? I knew I looked tired and I was awfully hungry, but not so much as to be eager for raw meat on unbaked bread dough! Which is pretty much what I told him. He shook his head and we laughed.

Not connecting one thing to the next -- it's a very human mistake. Sociologists tell us that living in our modern society, we, especially, have learned to "compartmentalize" our world, to separate each thing into its particular little box, like sorting mail for those rental boxes at the post office.

"This will get me ahead at work. It goes here." "I do this for the kids so it goes here." "This makes me feel good. I do this for me." "This is an investment for the future."

We sort and separate our choices routinely. But if we do not make connections between these categories, we, too, risk making some ridiculous mistakes. Read Jesus' parable in Matthew 18:27-28, for example.

"And out of pity for him, the lord of that slave released him and forgave him the debt. But that same slave, as he went out, came upon one of his fellow slaves who owed him a hundred denarii; and seizing him by the throat, he said, "Pay what you owe." When we need help, it's one thing, but when we think we're in control, it's a different story.

Now you know the bottom line here is going to be about God. The bottom line is the essential line, where it all makes sense. "In him (Jesus) all things hold together," we read in Colossians 1:17. When it comes to God, the same old patterns and categories just don't apply. We can't assume this is religious; this isn't, as if God has something to say about some parts of our lives and not about other parts.

The future, the present, the past – even with its failures – all things connect when you see them through Jesus' eyes. Your life, then, has purpose. And the purpose for your life connects with the purpose for my life. We connect. And the whole of this day – every decision, every conversation, every task – is more extraordinary than we might otherwise imagine when seen as a gift from the Lord who loves us!

Grace and Peace,
Pastor Shirley

Encounter, July 1996

"Heart to Hart" from the Pastor…

The doorstep was a small slab of cement tilted, no doubt, by the roots of a friendly tree nearby. A little girl sat on the tip of one corner, cradling the gray kitten which had rolled over onto its back and was patting the air with soft paws as she rubbed its tummy. She had tamed the kitten herself.

She was waiting for a ride, and sure enough, Aunt Kendra's blue car came bounding over the rain ruts in the driveway. It was time to go. "She's here!" the little girl shouted back at the doorway behind her and gently spilling the kitten into the grass jungle at her feet, she went to pull open the car door farther and get in. Today was the first day of day camp.

And so one came, and another and another. The grass was wet and someone fell, got up and looked at the palms of his hands to see if anything was broken, wiped them off by flattening and stretching the hem of his flapping tee shirt even a bit longer, and ran again.

One had a new hair ribbon and mom's carefully shaped curls. She was all pink and flowers. Even her shoes were pink. And her face was shy. She watched.

One knocked over his chair and the one next to him shouted, "That's cool, Scott." But it wasn't of course. Scott grinned. It was still morning. In the afternoon he would have had more to say back.

As they came, so did the noise. The one at the table couldn't be heard as she said her name so she had to say it again. The woman registering her looked up with a puzzled face to the taller sister or friend alongside for help. "Rachel. She's Rachel and I'm Angie."

A few parents stood at the end of the room, arms folded across their chests, wondering how this would go, wondering if they should leave, perhaps remembering other Bible School times when they had come home with hands full of papers and crafts and heads full of ideas themselves. Remembering how kids can push and shout and disagree loudly and want to be right. And then wondering, again, how it will go today and if they should leave yet.

And just then, someone, a leader, shouts "Hello!" And they all turn to look. And again, this someone shouts, **"Hello?"** This time it sounds something like a question. So some of them echo, "Hello!" **"Hello!"** "Hello"

This week I went to Day Camp, our version of Vacation Bible School. I could tell you about the creative crafts or about the way the kids listened to these teens who came all the way from Pennsylvania to teach the lessons this year. I could tell you about the nature walk that turned into the Zacchaeus story when someone noticed Bob up in a tree along the pathway or the cardboard village that inspired a spontaneous reenactment of the Good Samaritan story. (Have you ever seen our Lindsey with a full black beard?)

Day Camp was all of these things and more. I was so impressed with our guests, with their energy and smiles, with the way they attended to our kids, listening to them and helping them.

But most of all, Day Camp was this - the gathering of fifty or more kids from different homes, coming with different concerns, and different hopes, and becoming a community where they could find nurture for their lives and their souls. The kids wouldn't say it quite that way. They will tell you it was FUN! That's true! It was fun, the way fun is supposed to be! Good and healthy and right and Godly!

Thank God for this week!

Grace and Peace,
Pastor Shirley

Encounter, August 1996
"Heart to Hart" from the Pastor…

The village of Cavalier, like my own hometown, holds the county seat. Because of the stone turrets on the building's two front corners, it looks like a strong castle to the town's imaginative elementary children who walk past it on their way to school each day. Even at that early hour, they can see men and women dressed in suits, many carrying briefcases, turning up the walk and disappearing inside.

Spreading out like a web on either side of the river, the streets of Cavalier come into one another at multiple angles forming intersections that complicate driving considerably. As a result, out-of-town drivers are easily recognized by their frowns as they hesitate at these corners wondering who in the world has the right of way. Local folks just wave one another ahead, depending on who probably is in the biggest hurry to get where they're going. Folks pretty much go to the same places day after day, so that isn't too hard to predict.

And there on the river bank stands the Tannery. Ever since it cleaned up its act, business has begun to grow again. Not so much so that anyone in the area is wildly optimistic 'though. No, everyone, from the CEO, Clyde Harrison, to custodian Fred Tanner ("no pun intended," Fred often says) knows that the only way the factory will survive is for all of them to pull together, including working extra shifts and week-end overtime to meet whatever schedule the customers are demanding.

Of course, Cavalier has a "Main Street," which not unlike my own hometown, isn't actually called "Main Street," but rather "State Street." And for a few blocks, State Street is stately indeed. Along both sides as it approaches the castle-county building, the Beautification Committee of 1955 had planted Sugar Maples and now they tower overhead, sometimes lacy with spring-green buds and flora, other times supporting a heavy entanglement of leaves, whether forest green or dappled shades of gold, orange, or red. Even in winter, their powerful limbs hold gray skies at a distance.

The High School is lit up day and night during the winter months "because of all the sports and activities offered to kids these days," as Mary Ellen Nashfield is likely to explain to her customers at Mary Ellen's Fry House. But that hasn't been the only change in recent years. Now two health clinics have replaced Doc Bennett's office, and from above, Franklin's grocery must look like a club foot at the end of a skinny-legged strip mall. Besides these, there are the regular churches, a few insurance offices, the lumberyard, and the electric and gas companies.

That's the way life looks to Cavalier folks. And to their way of thinking, it makes sense to work long and hard, straighten things out in the courthouse, hire good teachers and coaches for their kids, follow doctor's orders when they are sick, and be friendly. Overall, their town is a strong, productive place, with enough trouble to keep those engaged in problem-solving occupations busy, and just enough heartache to make folks shake their heads over coffee. And sometimes come to church.

The castle hasn't crumbled. The basketball team is "going great guns!" (according to Mary Ellen, who should know because she hasn't missed a game.) And Cavalier, by the grace and patience of God, will, no doubt, remain cavalier, until Lord knows when.

Who sees anything wrong with this picture? Who pauses to ask, what is strength, really? Where does help come from? Who gives credit where credit is due anymore? When did congratulating ourselves and one another displace giving thanks to God? And does it matter?

I don't know about you, but questions like these make me wonder if it's time we take this story to Hart.

Grace and Peace,
Pastor Shirley

Encounter, September 1996

"Heart to Hart" from the Pastor…

I'd already maneuvered the car around corners to avoid State Street's barricades and now I slowly inched my way over new gravel flouncing out from the shoulders of Polk Road like the ruffles on a sun-colored smock top I once owned. A moment later I leaned with the car to make the last turn onto the expressway ramp much as I had leaned on my bicycle to coast across the seams of a sidewalk when rounding the corner of a city block when I was a girl or the way I hugged and leaned when riding behind John on his motorcycle some years later. Where are all these thoughts coming from, I wondered, finding the assortment mildly amusing.

From the past, silly, I replied idly to my own question. In my mind I could see myself moving through the years; coasting as a child, racing as a young woman, picking my way carefully and awkwardly when pregnant while trying to look cheerful about it in my "sunny" top. My mind wanders too much, I corrected myself, now looking over my left shoulder responsibly and merging my Buick into the next lane with only the slightest tilt of my hand.

"There," I breathed aloud. I reached for the radio buttons and cranked up the sound. On the move again, finally. No barriers, no traffic, no weather conditions, no hold-ups. Tuning in my regular channel, I even found a song I knew so, as I am likely to do, I began to sing along. Getting somewhere at last. This was the way I traveled these days: less carefree than in childhood, perhaps, and although sometimes finding life less exciting, surely also less weary and difficult than other times in the past. Over the years I've gained a sense of competence and ease, I guess.

With that thought, I entered the gap. Those of us who travel north-south or vice versa between Hart and Shelby all know the gap. It's the stretch of highway cut through the foredune that separates these two communities. Old 31 has Star Hill with its vistas, but the "new" road has a hard curve with recently seeded grassy sides wedging up and away from the road until reaching native woods at the top.

Once in the gap, I frowned. My radio station sputtered, flinging out half the words of my song and merging it with a strange baritone voice who was promising something I didn't catch because this too, in turn, was interrupted by static and then, a fancy guitar bridge. I frowned and pushed another preset button. Same problem. Again. Again the same mix of waning music and crackling static. Nothing comes in here, I thought, irritated.

Nothing comes in. Nothing satisfies. I'm frowning and frustrated when that happens to the radio. Interrupted just when I think I'm getting somewhere at last, when I'm finally able to cruise along.

Interrupted – like Karen with questionable results on her biopsy. Like Rosa whose married life had been routinely moral until the lint in the bottom of her dryer at home had caught fire and burned out the motor, making it necessary for her to take the kids' clothes to the laundromat where she met that handsome fella and her marriage suddenly became singed by sparks that flew between them.

Interrupted – like Bob who never seemed to get enough done in a day to satisfy himself anymore. Like Mark receiving a phone call saying his brother Ed had died of a heart attack after he'd mowed the whole lawn the day before without a single sign. Imagine that.

Static and dissonant sounds interrupting the beautiful music you had expected would play for you the whole way through. No matter how we've traveled thus far, how agile we are, how experienced, in the gap we all struggle to tune in something that makes sense. Yet, no matter where we turn the dial, everything is haywire.

Everything is haywire except the road before us. And when, for a moment, I forget to fret about the static, I notice that today the moth mullen has begun to bloom along the roadside, at eye-level in that ascending meadow, with melting yellow or blushing pink star-shaped pillows that unfold into simple smiling blossoms. And I tolerate the static better when I discover that, about at the halfway mark, the gap is crossed by another dune spur opening up a brief glimpse of cozy homes across the valley.

I get through the gap time and time again not on the strength of the past – for nothing in the past has prepared me for this – nor by focusing on and trying to fix my problems myself, but only, finally, by trusting that the road that led me in will also lead me out and by looking for unforeseen delights to sustain me meanwhile.

Our Lord has said, "I am the way."

How I move has always said a lot about who I am.

Grace and Peace,
Pastor Shirley

Encounter, October 1996
"Heart to Hart" from the Pastor…

My wandering eyes give me away. How about you?

For some of you, it's the faint beeping of the alarm on your digital watch. For others, it's a sort of code word or action. You shift your weight or stand up to stretch and say, "Well, I guess…"

"Let's get on with it."

"What's next?"

Restlessness. "Agenda anxiety" one of my friends calls it. It's the I-don't-have-all-day syndrome. "I have so much work to do." "We're really swamped." After all, I'm a busy person.

Some people offer hints of promises. "This is just temporary." "Things are going to change. They have to." And they smile apologetically.

Or some expect everyone to agree with them: "'Has to be this way. Work doesn't do itself, you know." And they shrug.

In our society, busy people are important people. And we all need to be important. But we also need to know what is important. Or rather, who.

To be fair, I think we DO say: "My kids come first." or "My husband comes first." (Frankly, I don't often hear, "My wife." The closest to that was a remark one fellow made at a meeting that was running late. "I don't want to keep her waiting. I messed up one marriage and I'm not about to wreck this one too." I guess that's something like, "My wife comes first.")

But that's about it. I have my priorities: work and family. Not necessarily in that order, but yes, sometimes.

Yet, when I say I'm busy working, everyone (including my family) is supposed to nod in agreement and forfeit any other expectation they may have been harboring for my time. After all, work is an irrefutable priority, or is it? Or work may be a different way of saying my family comes first, if we are sincerely working to afford to live and accomplish shared goals. But just as often work can be a way of saying, "I come first." Work can be a way of avoiding people, of avoiding commitment, of avoiding give-and-take. Working is just plain easier than relating.

If there's more to this than meets the eye, then what insight can our faith give us in our busy lives?

I know back in the first century, Palestine didn't have an interstate highway let alone an information highway, but Jesus was busy too. At one point, it seems you couldn't get an appointment with him no matter how hard you tried. Those who waited hoping to catch him en route between speaking occasions often were put off by his entourage of companions – young mothers who hoped this rabbi would bless their children, for example; or a blind man who had an irritating voice. It was hard to get to see Jesus. Maybe that's why a woman in the crowd grabbed the hem of his robe and a man once climbed a tree hoping just to lay eyes on him.

As far as family goes, on the one hand, Jesus loves his mother. He even lets her talk him into doing a favor for her at a friend's wedding in Cana. Later, during his own great physical and spiritual pain on the cross, he takes time to make sure she has someone to lean on.

But when it comes to priorities, Jesus doesn't automatically bless "family first" or a "me and mine" mentality. *"Who are my mother and my brothers?" he asked. Then he looked at those seated in a circle around him and said, "Here are my mother and my brothers! Whoever does God's will is my brother and sister and mother."* (Mark 3:33-35).

The will of God...it's the will of God that I love God with ALL my heart, soul, mind, and strength. That I worship.

It's the will of God that I focus on the human faces in front of me, that I give them priority over the face of my watch.

It's the will of God that I don't let self-importance and busyness displace either God or any of the persons God brings into my life each day.

Perhaps the next time I say "I'm busy" I should, at the very least, look embarrassed.

God's Grace and Peace,
Pastor Shirley

Encounter, November 1996
"Heart to Hart" from the Pastor...

In this place to speak from my heart to yours, I need simply to say "thank you" once again for the past five years. When Doug S. spoke about this anniversary last Sunday morning on your behalf, his words were kind and generous. My only thought was, "I wish I could live up to this." Sincerely, that's my heart's desire, to counsel you well in the ways of God.

The professor-friend who preached at my ordination five years ago chose Isaiah 6:1-8 as his text and brought us vividly to God's throne with its attending angels. In that vision, Isaiah, who is a priest, is overwhelmed by the holiness of our God and at the same time is deeply aware of his own unworthiness. However, an angel leaves God's side and rushes to Isaiah's lips with a burning coal so he can be forgiven. Then when God has a message for the people, Isaiah can be sent to speak to them. An artist friend of mine captured her impression of this angel for the cover of my ordination bulletin that day. Who could have known how surely your gift of another "angel" last Sunday morning would take me back to those moments when it all began for me? What a beautiful and meaningful gift! (Special TY to Jan, who picked it out!)

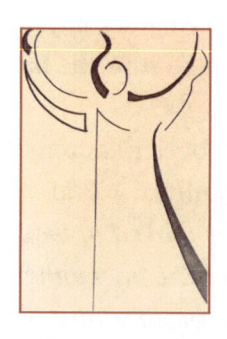

    Perhaps some of you have not seen the leaded-glass angel that I received as a gift from you. It must be all of a foot and a half high. This angel does not seem as static as the wings and robe of opaque pearl and gray glass might suggest because of an upturned face and arms that are outstretched. There's a sense of hope and joy and pronouncement about the movement. An angel of bright anticipation.

    But you should know that I had to move some things to suspend her in the window above my desk at home. For one thing, I had to take out the screen. And I had to take down the curtain. I even put away the grid that normally cuts the window into panes. "They were just fussy decorations blocking and filtering the light that tries to come in anyway," I thought, as I wiped away some dust. But, to be honest, I've grown so used to them that, even though the room was dimmer before, it also was more familiar and comfortable. Now I'm startled to see the angel there when I walk in. Yet, I do like the light.

99

That's a lot to consider. Of course, I'm not thinking about my window so much as about how, by putting something beautiful in my life, you've nudged aside some dusty old things that were already there. Your gift not only brought back memories, but it has also put me to work making some perhaps long-overdue changes. So, this morning I'm thinking again about how self-giving our Lord Jesus is and about us. I'm reminded that sometimes it takes a loving nudge before we open our lives to more light.

And all the while an angel stretches out her arms above my head.

Grace and Peace,
Pastor Shirley

Encounter, December 1996
"Heart to Hart" from the Pastor…

This is a time for making plans. As I sit here typing at my desk tonight, I can see the message light on my answering machine blinking to remind me that I have to get back to my sister-in-law about when we can celebrate the holidays together as a family. A pastor friend of mine made this observation the other day, "In December everyone always begins a conversation with me by saying, 'I know you're busy, Pastor, but…' What they don't know is that by the time December arrives, most of my work is done. It's in November that I'm really busy! That's when I do all my planning."

So you've caught me in the middle of making plans. One way I do this is by opening my Bible, digging into my files, and spreading everything out around me. All the while I'm trying to draw together themes, to name sermons, to choose hymns, to check dates just as I do this time every year. Yet, today in the middle of everything, the title of one small advent devotional booklet moved me the moment I saw it. The phrase was familiar and warmly inviting, but for a brief, puzzling moment I couldn't place the song that it was taken from. Do you recognize it? "Some would even say it glows" That's right! It's from *Rudolph the Red-Nosed Reindeer!*

Immediately my next thought was, "Why in the world would someone use part of *Rudolph the Red-Nosed Reindeer* as a title for a Christian devotional booklet?" There was a time when I could get pretty irate about things like that. I didn't want Frosty the Snowman or Santa or Rudolph to steal the manger scene. Furthermore, to my way of thinking, many non-religious activities like shopping and partying competed in threatening ways with the sacred story of that silent night.

It's not a new concern. From the earliest times in church history, the faithful have raised the same issue. Syncretism. What is lost if we blur the distinction between the secular and the sacred? What if we blend traditions? The transition from Judaism to Christianity raised those questions. Should Christians still observe Jewish dietary laws? What of Passover? Or circumcision? The Apostle Paul writes letter after letter trying to resolve the dilemmas.

Through centuries again and again the church reclaimed pagan holidays and infused them with Christian meaning. That was true of Easter, originally a pagan festival to mark the arrival of Spring. It was also true of decorations like the Christmas wreath and the lighted Christmas trees we all love. Light symbols were used in German folklore throughout November and December as the year's darkest days closed in. Yet, how beautifully they remind us that Jesus is the Light of the World.

But I'm pragmatic enough also to recall how my feet feel after shopping for a few hours in the mall, and how I shift my weight while waiting in line at the cash register for the umpteenth time while someone's check is being approved. I remember trying to hold a sweater up to the torso of a fidgeting, too-small child to judge if it would fit an older, bigger one. I remember wondering about the color, wondering if it was "cool" enough. I remember parties that weren't full of good cheer after all. But I still get disturbed by all the materialism, all the hassle and glitz that competes with the sacred story.

"Some would even say it glows…" – "some," surely those of us who embrace the amazing truth that God came to us in Jesus, in a non-threatening, humble way to draw us to himself – surely we would say, "it glows!"

And what "glows?" The glory of God bursting the seams of heaven, the appearance of angels fresh from God's radiant presence, the lantern in the stable, the hope of the ages, the truth -- it all glows, doesn't it?

"Even say" that it glows…among all the other things that we might say – all the re-telling of events, all the tracing of the movement of shepherds and wise men, all the calculation of the path of a star, all the searching of ancient prophecies for an exact location – more than the sum of these details, this story glows with God's promise come true!

As I thought further, it occurred to me that the line from the song perhaps applies in more significant ways to Jesus' birth than to any reindeer's nose. No comparison! This led me to wonder what else in our culture, in our world might be reclaimed for our Lord if we weren't so busy keeping our distance from it.

Then, I decided on a line from another secular song as the title for our Advent season here at the church. I'm hoping that by doing that we will be reminded to go into all the world and preach the gospel in ways that will transform the kingdoms of this world into the kingdom of our Lord!

Grace and Peace,
Pastor Shirley

(The theme I chose for this advent season was "Making Spirits Bright!" from "Jingle Bells." Theme verse: "I am...the bright morning star." Revelation 22:16b)

Encounter, January 1997
"Heart to Hart" from the Pastor…

    Words tumble over themselves in an attempt to express the thank-full-ness we feel toward our dear Evie for always being there at her "post" and "listening" to us so well through all these years.

    All who read the *Encounter* each month will miss the way she has regaled the changes in the seasons, the coming and going of birds at her feeder, the sprouting of a leaf, and the exact shade blue in the autumn sky.

    But most of all we have looked to her to find ourselves. And never did we find an accomplishment listed without an accompanying pat on the back, never a blunder recounted without the delightful ability to find life's humor in it. Evie N. has a gift for such things and she has been wrapping that gift in printed words for many years here.

Evie, the loss of your vision saddens us. Most of us can only imagine the changes that will mean for your life. You always have our loving support and prayers, you know.

And we want you to know how much we will miss your column. However, all along, writing has only been one of the many ways you have shared your gifts of encouragement and hope with us. You have always brightened the church with your smiles, your voice and laughter, your touch and hugs, (not to mention your delicious blueberry pies!) Nothing has diminished those!

To be recipients of your beautiful gifts nowadays, I guess the rest of us will just have to do what you have been urging us to do at the close of every one of your columns all this time: Come, join you in worshiping our Lord and sharing his love with others!

Grace and Peace to you, dear lady,
Pastor Shirley

[February 1997 missing]

Encounter, March 1997
"Heart to Hart" from the Pastor…
"They say…," I began, but I was interrupted immediately.
"Who are 'they'?" my friend asked.

It's a common mistake, not identifying the source of our frustration or the authority for the view we're expressing. Sometimes we can quickly repair the situation by simply naming who they are; yet, in some ways all "theys" are alike, aren't they?

"They" are always a group of folks and by their sheer number, they have more votes than, say, you or I alone or even both of us together.

And beyond that, "they" seem to have things under control, to be in the "know," as we say. They have it all figured out and what they have figured out often limits what we might think or do. They determine how we figure into things.

You might think such a powerful legion would leave quite a trail; yet, "they" are never around when you need them. They let others communicate their views for them.

Perhaps most of their power comes from being anonymous. Therefore, they cannot be reasoned with; their conclusions cannot be questioned or challenged.

"They have taken the Lord out of the tomb, and we do not know where they have laid him." It is the first Easter greeting.

Very likely Peter recognizes Mary Magdalene's voice even in the dark. Peter also probably has a pretty good idea who "they" are – guards working for the rest of "them," the religious authorities. He rushes ahead into the tomb, but Mary begins to cry.

Once the men have left, we hear the angels ask her, "Why are you weeping?" A moment later Jesus himself asks, "Woman, why are you weeping? Whom do you seek?"

I've heard many Easter sermons on that last question, "Whom do you seek?" But I can't remember ever hearing one on the first question, "Why are you weeping?" Maybe that's because we know why she weeps. "They" frighten us too.

They say sunshine searing through the torn ozone layer will destroy life on earth as we know it. They say we can't trust the government, or the media, or lawyers, or the police, or a nice guy asking for a date, or one another. They say we underestimate the influence of violence and pornography and corruption and drugs. For the first time in ages they say the next generation will not have a better quality of life than our own. In fact, today they are beginning to say the next generation may be clones of our own.

"They say it's cancer." "They say she has only a few months to live." "They say he'll never walk again." "They say there's no hope."

Still, Jesus asks, "Why are you weeping?" I think it's important to notice <u>when</u> he asks it – just after he arose from the dead. Notice, too, that now the question has completely shed its long tail of their answers.

On Easter we celebrate that, no matter what "they" may say, God has the last word. It's a redemptive word, a word of hope, of future, of forgiveness, of new life!

Come, celebrate with us!
Pastor Shirley

Church takes hope to another level

Sunday, March 16 bouquets of over 300 daffodils adorned the sanctuary of Hart Congregational United Church of Christ during morning worship.

Along with many other organizations and people in the community, members and friends of the church made donations to the American Cancer Society's spring daffodil fund raising campaign.

However, the bouquets they received were displayed to brighten the sanctuary as a witness to the church's commitment to stand with those who struggle with cancer.

"Cancer is so limited ... it cannot cripple love, it cannot shatter hope, it cannot corrode faith, it cannot destroy peace, it cannot kill friendship, it cannot suppress memories, it cannot silence courage, it cannot invade the soul, it cannot steal eternal life, conquer the spirit," said an anonymous poem read in unison by those attending the service.

Prayers of compassion for area cancer patients included thanksgiving for times of remission and expressed for longing for a cure. Sunday's service was the congregation's third annual event. Following worship, members delivered flowers to shut-ins and to Oceana County Medical Care Facility residents.

Encounter, April 1997
"Heart to Hart" from the Pastor...

"What do you want?" he asked. I was only 10 or 11 years old and he was my great-grandpa. He was the one living far away, with a scrawling style of handwriting that reminded me of one of the signers of the "Declaration of Independence" that hung next to the flag in my school room that year. Looking like one of those fellows too, as far as I could tell from the picture my mother had on the buffet in the dining room. Pure white hair, narrow rugged face, large sunken eyes.

But, soon it would be summer vacation and the first thing we were going to do as a family to celebrate our independence was to take a trip to Little Rock, Arkansas to see him! Since I was the one in the family that absolutely hung on the mailbox and sent replies by return mail, I also was the one who told him the news and I was the one who "heard" the happy anticipation in his response. I was the one to whom he made promises like this one: "When you come, I'm going to take you out to the Sterling Store here and you can pick out anything you want and I'll buy it for you. What do you want?"

No one had ever asked me that before. Not and meant it. Not in that tone of voice. Usually, I sounded more like, "Now what do you want?" and I was facing an impatient adult with a hand on one hip, foot-tapping, face frowning. "Put out," we said when we wanted to describe that stance. He's put out about being interrupted. She's put out about all the demands you make on her. They're put out with you.

Years later, having fallen in a kind of young love, a boyfriend asked me, "What do you want?" And still one to be quick to respond, I said, "Some of your time." The words surprised me too. I didn't know until I heard myself what it was that I wanted from him; yet, in a flash, I was sure of my answer. And he smiled (probably thinking he'd gotten off easy) and promised. A few months later, when my heart was broken, I came to understand what had happened in terms of that question and answer. "He didn't have time for me." "He didn't make time for us." When it comes to relationships, I'm still a learner. But over time I've become even more resolute about that early, impulsive answer. Relationships need time. They gasp without it.

The question (and its answers) has grown up with me. When I was a child, it seemed brand new, but since then, I've faced it again and again, especially in the timid eyes of people who don't dare to ask it out loud anymore. But I want to confess something. As many times as I've come to the question, "What do you want?" I don't often give the truest answer, the answer I know by heart. I told my grandpa that I wanted a doll and I got one with rooted hair. When I was a teenager, whenever an impatient adult asked, "Now what do you want?" I learned to answer, "Nothing." Other times, I just learned to deal with the reality of disappointment.

I know I'm not supposed to think of God as a doting grandfather, but deep inside, I'm hard to convince because of my great-grandpa's attention and his crazy, no-strings-attached gift. My mind danced, not so much to consider the options, but to discover a new tune! And from then on, I kept listening for its lovely strains in other relationships. Now and then I've heard them in the church.

In this season when we celebrate God's beyond-your-wildest-imagination Easter surprise, at a time when the sunshine makes our eyes water and songbirds and blossoms infect us all with the delirium of spring fever, when we look forward to more family get-togethers in the better weather ahead, in this beautiful season intertwined with relationships with God, with earth, and with each other, I want to pass along the answer Jesus gave me to that question. It's something I say with joy back to him and also something that I now can say with new energy to others because of him.

> Perhaps you already know?
> The best answer to "What do you want?" is...
> "To be with you."

Grace and Peace to You,
Pastor Shirley

Encounter, May 1997
"Heart to Hart" from the Pastor…

The little girl swings down the street, skipping feet, arms outstretched to catch the lamp posts one by one as she passes and spins around each of them first one way and then the other, dancing her own spring dance.

The car door won't open for some reason. Stuck. He turns his wrist to read his watch and gives the handle another exasperated jerk. It opens. Seconds later, he pulls out and is swallowed up in traffic.

Somewhere a bird calls. The spirea buds are leafing out, wearing only their yellower, springtime green coats as yet, but looking hopeful. Meanwhile, the wind blows a brown cluster of last year's leaves loose from a mattered pile in the hedge and it skitters along the sidewalk like a mouse.

Sometimes it seems that breezes only stir up delight in the creation itself and small children. We've noticed this. That's why I golf, pull weeds, and hang clothes on the line. And why my father fishes. It's why some people choose to work in construction rather than with computers. It's the reason many of us run or walk. And why we want an office with a window.

We miss the carefree dance or perhaps the almost-motionless unfolding of ourselves. Still, we get some joy and new energy from seeing that around us, and then we get back to work.

God has noticed this about us. As our choices work themselves out day by day, we could begin to wonder why we race around, why we never seem to be done, why we worry when life doesn't seem manageable. We could begin to wonder if our ways are all that healthy after all. When we see how God's Spirit blows all around us -- refreshing, cleaning, changing, bringing – we could choose to let it in. But do we?

Yes, when we are weary, God's ways appeal to us, but let us get our second wind and so many of us just throw ourselves back into the same old race with new vigor, don't we? We are still bent on going our own way, although now with God's help.

"You grow weary from your many wanderings, but you did not say, 'It is useless.' You found your desire rekindled and so you did not weaken," God tells his people (Isaiah 57:10). What doesn't weaken, I think, is our determination to rely on ourselves and our tendency to do things the way we want them done.

Because God is good, we can take advantage of that goodness. But everything that God touches shows us that life was meant to be so much more. "Look, you serve your own interest," says God. "Will you call this…a day acceptable to the Lord?" (Isaiah 58:3b, 5) Then he goes on to describe another way, a self-giving way. And the outcome of that way of life, the by-product perhaps, is satisfaction and childlike delight! "The Lord will guide you continually and satisfy your needs in parched places…and you shall be like a watered garden like a spring of water whose waters never fall." (Isaiah 58:11)

Not a drinking fountain, not a rest stop, but a way of life that is continually refreshed. I think we hesitate because we think being a Christian will mean living with less, but the truth is that God wants all the souls he created and loves to have much more peace and real joy than we settle for.

The church puts it this way:

Fair are the meadows,
Fairer still the woodlands,
Robed in the blooming garb of spring;
Jesus is fairer, Jesus is purer,
Who makes the woeful heart to sing.

Grace and Peace and spring in your step,
Pastor Shirley

Encounter, June 1997

"Heart to Hart" from the Pastor…

"My cup runneth over," says the author of Psalm 23. It's right there in the middle of the Bible, one of those lines we learned as children, a line we still murmur to ourselves every time we hear the old Psalm read aloud again, right? We may make other mistakes, like inadvertently omitting the part about being anointed with oil or putting "still waters" before "green pastures" rather than the other way around. And, except for Christmas pageants, I've never had much first-hand experience with a "rod" or "staff," have you? But cups are more familiar.

I can even picture this one in my mind. Hands cupped (as we say) around it, holding it out for someone to fill, feeling it grow heavier. Hearing the liquid gurgle up through the octaves from bass to soprano, singing as if it didn't have a care in the world. Then suddenly…it's spilling over the lip! Oo, wet bubbles are washing over the backs of my hands even as I hurriedly unclasp them. I shake the excess off one hand, while with the other I still struggle to cherish the cup so its contents won't be entirely lost. My stomach arches back instinctively. My arms thrust out. I gasp! What an unexpected delight! Cool, wet, and wonderfully surprising!

But, even as a child that picture made me sigh. You see, I knew that the "runneth over" part was supposed to be a good thing, but deep inside, I also knew I should resign myself to the fact that the "cup" part of this Psalm was probably just as stuck in Bible times as the shepherd was.

After all, if my cup ever had really "runneth over" I'd never hear the end of it. If my cup really "runneth over" someone was going to have to clean up all the mess. Probably me. "Weren't you looking at what was happening? Where was your mind anyway, girl?"

If my cup really "runneth over" someone was sure to cry over spilled milk. After all, someone had been careless. Someone was wasteful.

Or worse, someone was fooling around and not taking life seriously enough. That someone could count on a stern look, to say the least.

Yet, our God pours.

Robins and wrens and orioles, violets and forsythia and tulips. The softness of a grandchild's kiss, the most beautiful blue eyes you've ever seen, someone who trusts you. Possibilities when you come to a dead end. Perfect timing. Problems which turn out to be not that bad after all. (Whew!) Another day, another chance, another touch.

And always Someone to make a way for us, Someone to see us through. Our God pours himself out for us.

If bad things come in threes (as I've heard you say), surely good things come in three millions! So, why merely curl up under a wet blanket, or settle for dampened spirits when our God would drench us in love?

Much Grace and Peace,
Pastor Shirley

Hart Congregational United Church of Christ

408 S. State Street, Hart, MI
Office Phone 873-2449
Rev. Shirley Heeg

Worship Service 10:00 a.m.
NURSERY PROVIDED
Sunday School 11:15 a.m.
HANDICAPPED ACCESSIBLE
"Called to Care"

Encounter, July 1997

"Heart to Hart" from the Pastor…

Last week I attended the General Synod meetings for the Reformed Church in America in Milwaukee, Wisconsin. For all practical purposes, my dual standing in both the RCA and the UCC means that I attend twice as many denominational meetings as some of my colleagues.

Attending these meetings brings to mind a postcard my grandma sent when she traveled to San Francisco one summer. She had chosen a view of Alcatraz, the island prison, but across the bottom corner of the picture were the words, "Wish you were here!" We laughed because my grandma obviously hadn't caught on to that joke. But sometimes when I say I wish everyone here could attend more church meetings like the ones I attend, I get the impression that I might just as well have cheerfully invited all of you to prison!

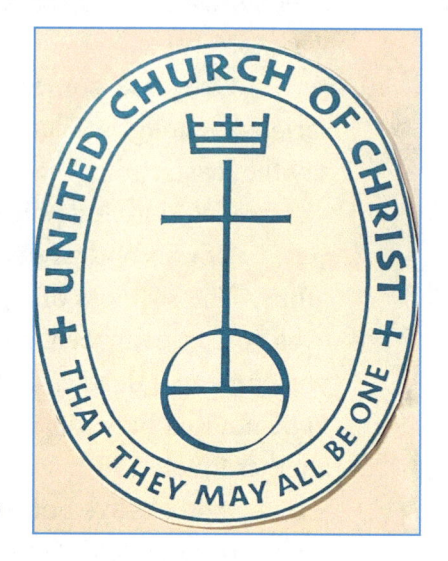

I do, however, wish you could have been there. All of you. Any one of you. Whenever I attend association, conference, or even national church meetings, I'm once again filled with awe at what it means to be the body of Christ together.

The key inter-church issue that the Reformed Church Synod faced last week was whether or not to sign a formula of agreement with the Evangelical Lutheran Church of America (ELCA). I was assigned to work with a committee that would bring a recommendation on the formula to the whole body later in the week.

This decision would end 400 years of differences and separation. It would be deliberated by four denominations. Some people in the Reformed Church in America were also using this occasion to raise concerns about ties with the UCC because of differences in the two church's official statements on homosexuality, and consequently, their suspicions about the way the UCC interprets the Bible.

Sitting on the committee while this debate took place was quite an experience! I've described some of that to several of you since I returned, but I wanted to take this space to highlight one particular and very special person I met during that time. His name is Rev. John T. and he is an ecumenical officer for the UCC who was attending these RCA meetings as a consultant. In that role, he sat in the same room as I did and listened as the discussion became increasingly heated and angry pronouncements were being made about the UCC. In fact, as our work concluded, the group officially voted to apologize to Rev. John T. for the "strident" language used in our arguments.

I remember, then, watching him as he stood to respond. I heard him calmly describe how much pain he had felt as he heard the church of his baptism, the church that nurtured his faith, the church that had called and ordained him, the church he loved – the UCC – presented in such negative terms. Yet, then, in quiet tones, he went on to assure us that an apology was unnecessary because, he said, people in the UCC are not threatened by strident language or hard debate. "In fact," said Rev. John, "we welcome it. Such openness could even be said to be characteristic of our denomination."

I wish you could have heard him. He's a soft-spoken man, but I also noticed that everyone quiets down to listen when he speaks. He's a tall man; still, when you think of his stature, his character stands out as surely as his height. I wish you could have been there because he represents us, the UCC, very well. He is the UCC at its best – diplomatic, accepting, clear about essentials, a good listener, a man of faith. All very impressive. Yet, perhaps most of all, I was deeply impressed with this: when hurt, he responded with grace and forgiveness.

The apostle Paul writes, "See that none of you repays evil for evil, but always seek to do good to one another and to all." (1 Thessalonians 5:15)

One of my souvenirs from these synod meetings is a new Bible, but I also came away with a new picture of how God's Word looks when it's lived out.

I wish you could have been there!

Grace and Peace,
Pastor Shirley

Encounter, August 1997
"Heart to Hart" from the Pastor...

What's Ahead? During the past few months, I have quietly presented this question to the boards and committees of this congregation: **What do you believe our church should be doing, especially as we approach the turn of the century?** Now as our annual meeting is coming up, I lay the same question before all of you for your prayerful consideration.

Once again, it's time to say clearly where we're headed. To name where we understand God's Love to be guiding us. Then to assess our resources, to focus our commitment toward meeting these goals, that is, to take Faith. And to start in the right direction together, with that characteristic Christian optimism called Hope!

Struggling with this question is important, but as you and I do this, we need to keep a few things in mind, I think.

First, it's important to understand that this isn't just a "make work" suggestion. I'm not asking for more projects to fill our time.

Second, it doesn't require us to reinvent the wheel. Our direction is not up for grabs, so to speak. We have stated our common mission. You probably recognize it readily or have it on hand. It's printed on page 2 of our pictorial directory and it hangs on the wall in the front entrance to our church building.

> **Our mission is to be**
> **An accepting congregation,**
> **Celebrating new life in Jesus Christ,**
> **Inviting others to faith**
> **Caring for one another**
> **Giving generously, and**
> **Committing our lives to be shaped**
> **By God's word.**

We have already seen many expressions of these guiding principles in the past five years. We support Good Samaritans with our contributions and volunteer hours. Together we pool our efforts for Cancer research, for Cystic Fibrosis, for Habitat. We have organized and provided space and support for the Oceana Parkinson's Support Group. We have hosted grief recovery courses, now available at St. Gregory's.

For families, the church provided a parenting course.

Parenting class offered at Hart Congregational

HART — Hart's Congregational United Church of Christ is offering a parenting class for parents of children ranging from birth through adolescence. The course will meet on four consecutive Monday evenings, Jan. 18 through Feb. 8, at the church parish house (across from the Hart Public Library), from 7 to 8:30 p.m.

Lee Noffke, nationally recognized psychologist, lecturer, and small group leader will conduct the series. The program will address the specific questions of those attending and will offer techniques to help them become better parents. Topics will include self-esteem, discipline, communication and more.

Noffke, a Pentwater resident, earned a bachelor of arts degree at the University of Utah and a master of arts degree at California State University. Her master's thesis and work with preschool education and parenting groups in the Los Angeles area earned her the Kelly Keogh Award. Now retired, Noffke taught for California State University at Northridge, Santa Monica College and The World University. She has served extensively as a discussion leader and counselor and has acted as psychological consultant to schools and corporations.

All parents, male, female, single or together, are welcome to attend the class. Child care will be provided in the church nursery. ◊

We were the first and perhaps only area church to provide the community a forum for discussing issues of trust and safety when children are in the care of church leaders and we provided a psychologist-led program on this issue for our own Sunday School children.

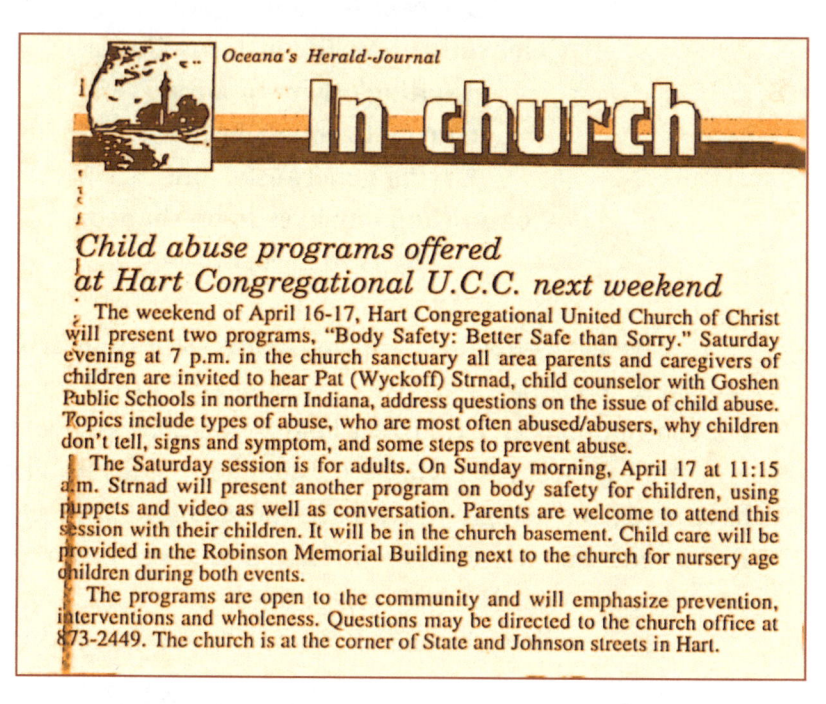

> *Oceana's Herald-Journal*
>
> **In-church**
>
> **Child abuse programs offered at Hart Congregational U.C.C. next weekend**
>
> The weekend of April 16-17, Hart Congregational United Church of Christ will present two programs, "Body Safety: Better Safe than Sorry." Saturday evening at 7 p.m. in the church sanctuary all area parents and caregivers of children are invited to hear Pat (Wyckoff) Strnad, child counselor with Goshen Public Schools in northern Indiana, address questions on the issue of child abuse. Topics include types of abuse, who are most often abused/abusers, why children don't tell, signs and symptom, and some steps to prevent abuse.
>
> The Saturday session is for adults. On Sunday morning, April 17 at 11:15 a.m. Strnad will present another program on body safety for children, using puppets and video as well as conversation. Parents are welcome to attend this session with their children. It will be in the church basement. Child care will be provided in the Robinson Memorial Building next to the church for nursery age children during both events.
>
> The programs are open to the community and will emphasize prevention, interventions and wholeness. Questions may be directed to the church office at 873-2449. The church is at the corner of State and Johnson streets in Hart.

Currently, our church is the training site for Rainbows, a peer group program for children of divorce or who have experienced the death of a parent. Again, members from our congregation have responded to the call to be a coordinator and facilitator for this project and soon children will be meeting here after school to work through their losses in a place where others listen with patience and compassion.

We provide a time of worship at the Medical Care Facility each month and one of our dedicated members volunteers more hours there than anyone else in the county. We pledge and walk for CROP and another member of our congregation coordinates this area-wide effort.

We held a series of Christian Living Lectures with guest speakers chosen for their ability to integrate faith and vocation. Members of a prayer group meet weekly to pray faithfully for the needs of our community, not merely our own concerns. A men's group also meets regularly to lift prayer concerns.

This is the Hart Congregational United Church of Christ behind the scenes. Of course, we worship, we teach, we sing, we donate, earn and distribute funds and goods through our committees and boards as always. Yet, now and then, I'm reminded that as pastor here, I'm in a position to see the church in ways that are invisible to other folks. All that goes to say, when I ask a question like the one I'm presenting here, not only am I expecting projects for committees, but also, and perhaps especially, I'm hoping that we will envision and commit ourselves to more of these sorts of efforts.

General William Booth, who founded the Salvation Army and who saw the beginnings of our century, shared this one-word mission statement with the organization: "Others." As I look over our efforts and our own mission statement with words like "accepting," "celebrating," "inviting," "caring," "giving," and "committing," it seems clear that we also are a people who demonstrate our love for our Lord by loving "others."

So how do you see that love taking shape in the years ahead? You are invited to submit your ideas in writing to the church office or any board member.

Let's take joy in discovering together where God is leading us!

Grace and Peace,
Pastor Shirley

Encounter, September 1997
"Heart to Hart" from the Pastor…
Read with me, would you?

I know it's time for school to start. Believe me, I know! I know about shopping trips and hauling furniture to a college dorm halfway across the state. I know about printing my name and address legibly on enrollment cards. (Through the years and to date, by my count, I have filled out 49 of them for our children!)

I know about doctor appointments and waiting rooms all too well. I know about sitting around the table for lengthy business meetings, even in the church. I know about civic responsibilities and volunteering. I know about walking, swimming, and aerobics. I know about groceries and bills. I know about diets (on this point, again, believe me, I know!)

I know about interruptions. I know about worries: about money, about being ignored, about pain, about things not going right at all.

Mostly I know that something will come up. Something always comes up!

Our lives are cluttered. But like the clutter in my closets, in the garage, on my counters, or on my desk, I also know that I'm not likely to get rid of any of these activities anytime soon. This is, after all, the bulk of my life.

Still, when I'm honest with myself, I also know how it feels to long for more profound things, for what is right and good, for closeness, for self-respect and peace of mind.

And I know the sort of sigh that most of us sigh whenever those things come to mind. I think we sigh because we know this is the important stuff of life and because sometimes we're not all that sure whether, in the end, we're really living our lives well.

Do you know there's a way to find out?

I don't know about you, but whenever I get like this, when I get caught up in everyday things without going deeper, I know it's time to open the book and hear Jesus again. So that's what I'm going to do these next few weeks. I'm going to listen to what Jesus has to say. Read with me, would you?

Read what Jesus says and does. Read Matthew who begins way back with the family tree and with the Christmas story. Read it out of season. Or read Mark, short, urgent, and to the point, a point the disciples almost miss. Luke tells his story with warmth and compassion. John tells it with awe and authority.

Now and then I hear someone use this modern-day quip, "Show me the money!" Did you know there is a spiritual version of that request? The disciple Philip brought it up to Jesus one day. "Show us the Father," he asks. Jesus answers him this way, "Anyone who has seen me has seen the Father." (John 14:9) To draw close to Jesus is to draw close to God.

But, in the same breath, Jesus also has said something that stops me in my tracks, "Have I been with you all this time, Philip, and still you do not know me?"

Good question.

In the midst of whatever you're doing these days, won't you take some time to read along with me?

The grace of our Lord Jesus be with your spirit,
Pastor Shirley

Encounter, October 1997
"Heart to Hart" from the Pastor…

Jim's golf game wasn't up to par (or perhaps "down to" par would be more apropos considering the direction his score would have to be headed in order to come even close!) He had had a good game through the fifth hole and by that time he pretty much had taken for granted that his swing would be consistent and he'd finish out the first nine with a respectable score. It didn't; he didn't. In any case, after hitting a wild hook where the fairway dog-legged to the right, he was more than a little frustrated with himself. Some fellows blamed the game of golf itself, saying that the serenity of the course and the simplicity of its goal were deceptive. Golf in itself is inherently frustrating. Some guys blamed their clubs and continually dreamed of newer ones, heavier putters, or Big Berthas. He blamed himself. He was a terrible golfer. "No talent," he said. "No patience." But he never said, "No hope." He was the sort that tried harder. The worse he played, the harder he tried. When the game got tough, he became more determined, but he did not become a better golfer.

Sue was on a diet again. Just this morning at work, Frances and Karen were moaning about how they could hardly believe it was fall already; the summer had been so cold and rainy that it barely seemed to be here and it was over. She overheard them talking, but she hadn't said what was on her mind. A cold summer meant she didn't have to wear shorts so often or feel like an elephant in her bathing suit at the beach. But here was a new season: a cooler, covered-up season, which meant that she now had three months to lose weight before the Christmas holiday parties. And Christmas photographs. So she was on a diet again. She would try harder this time. But inside, she wondered if she would ever be thinner.

Persistence is a valued character trait, one we like to find in people. Especially in workers, or athletes, or marriage partners. "Don't give up," we say to our kids. "Don't be a quitter." "You can do it!" a storybook voice still chugs along in our minds. You can do it if you think you can! "If at first you don't succeed, try, try again." You might succeed, but then again, chances are that you might just get awfully tired. With good intentions, I think, we persistently turn life into work. Day by day, we try hard. When others fall to the side, we lose respect for them. When we can't keep up the pace or accomplish what we set out to do, we feel useless and have less self-respect.

Yet, what if we were to rest? Like God did on the sabbath. Like Jesus did, while his companions battled the storm at sea.

What if we were to rest like God's people have always rested? Did you know that a newly married Israelite man was not to "be charged with any business for one year; he shall be free to be at home and shall be happy with his wife" (Deut. 24:5)? What if we were to try "not-trying" for a change?

I love to drive. I like to feel like I'm getting somewhere. But before I learned to drive a car, I drove our family speed boat, and that's a very different sort of driving experience – a better one in some ways, I'm inclined to think, because there, in the boat, when I finally had the sense to stop churning up the lake and shut down the engine for a few minutes, I began to notice something. Every time I pulled back the throttle to idle, the wake would have a chance to catch up with me and invariably, I felt its rising, lifting movement beneath me, gently rocking me.

And when I had the good sense to shut down completely, I could hear the water lapping all around me, at my side. I was afloat and buoyant. It hadn't been my speed that had been sustaining me all along, but rather the faithful waters.

I know the season for boating is pretty much past, but there's always walking, or maybe just stopping to breathe deeply. It's a good antidote for stress. And how especially wonderful for the soul! Faith, you see, is not a matter of trying harder.

"Be still and know that I am God," (Psalm 46:10)

Grace and Peace,
Pastor Shirley

Encounter, November 1997

"Heart to Hart" from the Pastor…

After Sunday service one morning, I remember one of the children asking, "Pastor, does everything remind you of God?" I guess that's what one might assume after weeks of watching me select object lessons each relating the gospel in one way or another. Surely, many things, perhaps all things, must remind me of God. I wish they did.

In truth, almost all of the reminders in my life are about things that I have to do. Some of these are obvious to anyone dropping in, like notes I've scribbled on a sticky tab and pasted to my computer screen, or a blinking light on the telephone answering machine. Some, I've discovered, only I can recognize: an empty cereal box on the counter reminding me to get groceries, for example. (Once John shook the Cheerios box and, thinking it sounded like it held enough for another serving, poured the contents into his bowl only to discover some pieces of cardboard, a few staples, and an orange peel I'd stuffed inside! That incident reminds me to throw empties away and take the time to write "cereal" on my grocery list instead.)

Most of the reminders in my life carry two messages; what to do, and, what seems equally important, to do it now or sooner. To hurry. Getting ready in the morning, or on my way to anywhere, the thoughts running through my mind most frequently sound like this: "I should have been there yesterday," "I should have done this last week," "I'm behind."

And at this point, I find little sympathy in the Book I carry. No matter what chapter I read for my morning devotions, no matter where I turn to read as I sit at someone's bedside making a hospital call, no matter what passage I've selected to study for Sunday worship, I have discovered again and again that what so often preoccupies me – being late, getting things done quickly, packing it all in – just does not seem to be a very prominent theme in Scripture.

The Scriptures talk of the fullness of time, but not just busying yourself with activities, rather the fullness of God. We sense here that completion has more to do with quality than deadlines. God's plan of salvation unfolds unhurried. In Galatians 4:4 we read. "But when the fullness of time had come, God sent his son, born of a woman...in order that we might receive adoption." Fullness has more to do with character than calendar. Of our Lord we read, "In him, all the fullness of God was pleased to dwell and through him, God was pleased to reconcile to himself all things." (Colossians 1:19-20) This doesn't mean there is no urgency in God's word, for that's there too, but the urgency has more to do with the need to understand and consider what direction to go before you head out the door. Paul reminds us, "Do this, understand the present time. The hour has come...your salvation is nearer now than when you first believed...so let us put aside the deeds of darkness and put on...light." (Romans 13:11-13)

According to the calendar, it's the time of the year that the leaves have to fall. In fact, it's a little late! But according to the design of their Creator, they don't just efficiently detach and drop one day; they take time to change color and delight us beforehand. They curl and catch the wind; they crisp and crunch underfoot, releasing the most wonderful aroma. Or they linger to catch the first coat of snow!

They remind me of God.

As Thanksgiving approaches and we begin to make other holiday plans as well, no doubt our calendars and our tables will soon be full. May that fullness also (and especially) be true of our hearts.

Grace and Peace,
Pastor Shirley

After the fall,
Time topples forward
To these nameless men
Who share their identity
With the sheep they tend,
Distant relatives to
The namer of sheep
Walker with God
Adam, the first.

Jarred abruptly from their watch
They tumble downhill
Hearts still throbbing
To the sweet, startling thunder
Of angelic chorale.

In the sacrament
At mangerside
The image
At last beholds
Its face.

With ancestral recognition
They sprawl upon
The earthen floor
And solemnly whisper
"Immanuel."

In this miracle moment
As the baby
God-Shepherd
First hears His name
The completion piece
Of the ancient
Hope puzzle
Falls perfectly
Into place.

SH

Christmas Letter   December 1997
Dears Friends,

Just a personal note here to wish each of you a beautiful Christmas season. It seems a little early to say "Merry Christmas" and, to be truthful, the word "merry" hasn't always fit the way I've felt about Christmas all that well. I didn't feel very merry the first few Christmases after my Mother died, for example. Or when an unexpected winter storm canceled our plans to get to family gatherings!

Still, regardless of circumstances, Christmas can always be beautiful. Candlelight is beautiful. Snowflakes are beautiful. I have beautiful memories of my Mother. Cuddling in a warm blanket when a storm winds whistle outside creates a beautiful, cared-for feeling. Even the sound of your own voice singing "Silent Night" is beautiful. (Yes, it is!)

And the old, old story is beautiful. Being close to our loving Lord is a beautiful experience for our souls. One we long for. Sometimes, when I stop to think, I marvel that what is truly beautiful about Christmas costs us so little, although it cost our God so much. "Christ Jesus…though he was in the form of God, did not count equality with God a thing to be grasped, but emptied himself, taking the form of a servant," we read in Philippians 2:6-7. "For God so loved the world that he gave his only begotten son," we read in John 3:16. May the beauty of Christmas in all its shapes and forms surround and delight you this year.

Once again John and I want to thank you for the love with which you have surrounded us and our children this past year. With Meri's diagnosis of diabetes, Elyse's illness this fall, and John's father's death, among other things, we have deeply appreciated your concern, your support, and your prayers. May God bless each of you in the year ahead.

"Glory to God in the Highest!" And to you, "Peace."
John, Pastor Shirley, Elyse, Anne, Aaron, and Merileigh

SHARING THE DECISIONS OF OUR HEARTS

December 1, 1997
Dear Members and Friends,

"Grace to you and peace from God the Father and our Lord Jesus Christ." Each Sunday morning I begin worship here with those words and each month I close my article in the newsletter with the same words. Grace and peace. They feel like the parenthesis within which I continually serve and speak with you. And they are the parameters within which I want to place this next bit of news as well.

On Sunday evening, November 16th, the congregation of the Church of the Savior in Rochester, Minnesota, voted to call me to be their pastor. That means John and I have a decision to make in the next few weeks.

We would deeply appreciate your prayers as we seek to understand God's direction for our family. I realize that this comes at a difficult time, just as we enter the Advent season together, and one of my concerns is that it will distract us from our primary focus, the celebration of the birth of our Lord Jesus. I don't want that to happen. That's why, God willing, I plan to announce my decision during worship on December 14.

I know I can count on your love and prayers. I hope you feel free to talk with me about this as well. Your thoughts are important to me.

As always, Grace and Peace,
Pastor Shirley

**Hart Congregational
United Church of Christ**

408 State Street • Hart, Michigan 49420 • (616) 873-2449

Shirley M. Heeg, *Pastor*

December 10, 1997

Dear Members and Friends,

    During the past month, as you know, John and I have been deciding how to respond to a call to minister at Church of the Savior in Rochester, Minnesota. We deeply appreciate your concern for our family and your faithful prayers for God's direction in this process. This congregation has always been and continues to be a blessing to us and that has made the decision all the more difficult. We have, however, decided to accept this call to ministry at Church of the Savior, believing it is God's will for us. We trust in God's care for all of you in this time of change. We will miss you.

As always, God's Grace and Peace,
Rev. Shirley Heeg

RE-ENCOUNTERING

After living and serving in Rochester, Minnesota for several years, I reconnected with Mary S., whom I knew well from my time at the church in Hart. She was a lively and bright personality, always inquisitive, quick to share her thoughts – a journalist through and through. We laughed easily together, but also talked seriously because she had come to Mayo Clinic in Rochester for medical treatment for advanced cancer. She returned many times because this process took years. At the beginning of summer, 2013, John and I were planning to move back to Michigan. I knew that meant I would be less available to spend time with her whenever she came to Rochester for appointments and treatments. So, we talked about how we could stay close, perhaps traveling back and forth together. We also talked about what it would be like for me to restart my life in Oceana County again after so many years away. I remember she dismissed my qualms with a laugh. "I'll make sure everyone knows you're back," she said. "You won't have any trouble reconnecting." Over the 4th of July holiday, John and I put our house up for sale and drove to Benona for vacation. Surprisingly, our house sold in 4 days. But I had even more of a jolt on July 13th, only a week later, when I found myself at Hart Congregational church once again, speaking at Mary's memorial. Her death saddened me, and yet, for a moment as I looked out across the large number of people who had gathered for the service, I couldn't help but think of her promise to reconnect me with the community. And her delight when a good story came together like that.

Not long afterward, on November 15, HUCC Pastor Lorraine B. died unexpectedly while attending a beautiful concert in town. What a shock for the members of the church! They had a deep loss to absorb and very little time to readdress what worship would be like in two days. I remember the phone conversation I had with

Denny on Saturday morning. We decided to proceed with the worship bulletin that Pastor Lorraine had set out, to sing the hymns she had chosen, and then I would moderate a time when the congregation could share memories and pray.

Shortly afterward, the church asked if I would step in as an interim while they sorted out their next steps. I was reluctant to take on a full-time position again, but agreed to share the ministry with another part-time pastor. We began almost immediately and over the next few months, I wrote the following newsletter articles.

May 2014
An Encounter... with the Wind of Pentecost
    The other day I walked out to the mailbox barefooted. That seems like a simple sentence, doesn't it? But for those of us who have been waiting for Spring to arrive in west Michigan, it borders on astounding! The ground was soft, but chillingly cold in the shadows where it was still wet with dew so as you might imagine, I hurried.
    In the mailbox, I found another nice surprise, the latest issue of a magazine I enjoy. I thumbed through it as I walked back toward the house. Finding an article I wanted to read, I looked around for a place to sit outside. By now my feet were wet and aching from the wind so I decided to curl up on the "hot" cement by the garage door. The sun felt terrific and it was so bright that the letters on the magazine page seemed to waver and change from black print to rosy-purple. When I finished reading, I leaned back against the door with my face up-tilted in the sunlight to think.
    I thought about how I am always quick to say I love being outdoors, but what I actually mean is that I love basking in warm sunshine and feeling all toasty and comfortable in the reflected heat radiating around me. Wind can irritate me. It doesn't leave

me alone, disturbs my pages, and chills as it evaporates whatever is damp and drear.

The wind – ruach, in Hebrew -- what a fitting image for God's Spirit! That wind is powerful enough to usher in a new season in our lives. Moving, changing, disturbing, recreating -- and also, maybe -- beautiful to observe through glass windows? Sure I love being with God, I always say, but maybe what I actually mean is that I love basking in the warmth of grace and feeling all "comfy" in the loving fellowship of those around me. Do I let God move me into unfamiliar territory, and change me dramatically? When it comes to ruach, how often do I have cold feet?

Pastor Shirley

July, 2014
Encountering others…

Last week, the clerk at the auto parts store saw me sitting in the truck, waiting outside while John was at the counter buying some oil so he sent an Avon sales booklet out with him for me. Hmm, I thought. I've given up trying to figure out why someone would do that long ago. (Unless I'm trying to be funny. Then I'm likely to pull down the visor mirror to see how bad I must look for someone subtly to suggest Avon in that way!) The truth is this is just the sort of place we live. People notice each other, offer things, and connect.

On the other hand, while some of our stores have automatic doors, we don't go in much for automatic "hellos." As far as I know, our local grocery stores don't employ greeters to say hello to everyone indiscriminately. If someone says hello to me, I usually look up to see a familiar face.

Now an outsider might think these two shopping stores cancel each other out. They don't of course. Both have happened around here and both seem somewhat sensible to those of us who live here.

When I first moved to Oceana County, years ago, I was often surprised or puzzled as I encountered new situations. I'm guessing some folks just shrug it off or don't look back as they pass by. But I like it here and I wanted to stay and belong, so I was determined to learn the ins and outs.

Tonight I spent some time south of Haran, on my way to Shechem with Abram. I've been reading chapter after chapter of Genesis. I wanted to understand what he was thinking. How did he make sense of this long journey and all of God's promises that remained just that – unfulfilled promises for a very long time?

And that made me think how easy it would be to jump to conclusions and assume I understood this ancient man and his walk with God. In Abram's case, I'm not just moving up north a few counties; I'm crossing oceans, centuries of time, language barriers, and gender gaps! And yet, getting to know Abram is important to me because Abram encounters God, our God. If I misunderstand Abram – or Sarai or Ruth or Jeremiah or Matthew or Peter or Paul -- I can't recapture their experience with the Lord clearly. And that would be my loss.

We begin to understand others when we spend time with them.
    We grow close to others when we spend time with them.
    True of our daily lives.
    True of those we meet in the Bible.
    True of our relationship with God.

Blessings along the way,
Pastor Shirley

August 2014

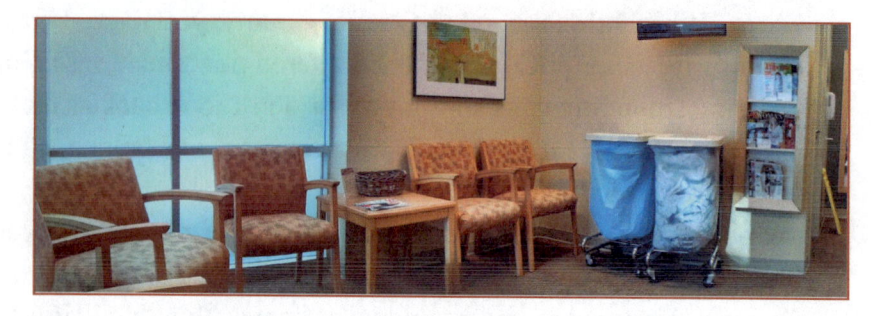

Encounter with my very own cancer…

I've encountered IT before, cancer I mean. But it's always been someone else's cancer. This summer, it's been mine. Last night when John and I were eating supper near the open windows with that balmy Big Lake breeze wafting inland to our place. I couldn't help but think back to this past winter. "Remember how cold, how long, how snowy it was then?" I asked. "Back then I thought this summer would be so wonderful compared to such a terrible winter." However, the summer had barely begun when I was diagnosed. And I soon discovered that cancer sets such a high score in the bad-news category that previous bad days hardly seem worth mentioning by comparison.

I was also surprised by another discovery. After years of thinking of myself as rather indecisive much of the time, I found out that I can be extraordinarily decisive when faced with something as jarring as cancer. Suddenly I had an instant motivator for re-prioritizing my life. Not that all my old choices were bad; they weren't. But almost immediately, it became very clear to me that I was paying a lot of attention to things that merely filled up my time without adding much real value to my life. Enough of that! So I unceremoniously dumped what wasn't worth my time and, believe it or not, I almost felt physically lighter. Easiest diet I've ever been on – a "spiritual" cleanse, of sorts – and the best part was that I didn't even have to whip up something green and kale-ish in my blender and convince myself to drink it!

I hope I've learned a lot these past three months. I think I may have. I've been reminded again how much closeness matters. I earnestly sought out closeness to God. In church services, I listened for words to remember later while waiting in the doctor's office. I copied down a verse from a hymn and sang it silently. I covered some familiar faith ground by thinking again how grateful I am that Jesus came to live among us. I need the kind of God who would do that to convince me I'm not alone and that my fears and troubles are known and cared for. I did not want God to be distant.

I also wanted closeness with those whose faces are so beautiful to my way of thinking that I almost tear up just bringing them to mind, my own loved ones. And then, at the same time, I found myself more acutely aware of suffering people. For me, one of the more amazing things about coming into the cancer center for treatments day after day has been seeing others who are going through the same things or something even more challenging. They smile, they talk quietly to one another, they hold the door open, wait patiently in lines, and even work on a jigsaw puzzle on a table together. In some ways, I think we are all puzzling our way through.

I've learned something about my deep-down, bottom-line belief about prayer too. It started with some practical questions early on: who needs to know? How will I tell them? Again, I was surprised at my own reaction. I didn't feel the need to be on a massive number of prayer lists. (I'm currently connected to four congregations in four different denominations. Trust me, I could summon prayer partners like Jesus could summon angels!) However, especially in those first few days when I was waiting for answers to very scary questions, I longed for private, heartfelt prayers, not necessarily numbers of them. I'm not so sure that God is impressed with volume as much as quality. I was confident in the group I turned to. However, I soon realized that their lives weren't carefree at the moment either. So, we began praying for each other. I don't think I've ever fully appreciated the bond that comes from giving AND receiving prayers like this before. It levels the ground and lifts my spirit.

I have learned that I love life. I like the look of a delicate cosmos blossom and marvel that my dahlias are so huge and gorgeous, although they are grown from tubers that I stuffed into ground that hadn't been tilled in nearly two decades. I love the softness of skin and the sound of familiar voices. I love the gift that life is and at the same time, I grieve that for some here on this earth, life is incredibly brutal or endlessly bleak. That troubles me more than cancer does.

When people ask how I'm doing, I usually say something about being grateful for good news, about the outcomes of tests and where I am in the process, but that's not the half of it really, you know. God is close. I am blessed and I marvel. I pray and I'm not afraid. I am not alone. I am loved. I can share what truly matters. And although none of this is news, it is all so very fresh and new to me today because cancer passed my way.

Pastor Shirley

Report for Annual Meeting, September 16, 2014

Greetings and blessings – Those might be common words to begin an article for a report like this one (or a letter like the ones we read in the New Testament), but, for me, they're also words that describe the welcome I've experienced here this past year. I'm grateful to be here.

I'm also grateful for the opportunity to write a few words for this annual report to describe what I am observing when I am among you. You all know the church from the "inside out," including many ways that I'm sure I am missing, but hopefully, I can offer some observations from the perspective of someone who has stepped back "in" after several years away.

First, it's good to see you. You smile easily, especially as more time has passed since Pastor Lorraine's death. It has been obvious from the start that she was as dear to you as you were to her.

You regularly gather prayers with a "wideness" that reminds me of the title of the old hymn, "There's a Wideness in God's Mercy." You not only are concerned for each other and your extended families, but also for Hart, the surrounding area, and the broader world.

Your weekly announcements include community events, not merely activities held here in the church building. That tells me that your presence on this corner remains significant and vital. You step up, pitch in, and respond when needed. In other words, you do not only exist primarily for yourselves but also for others. That is a basic marker for the health of a congregation.

If, at this time, from my limited role here, there's a place for direction or nudging forward, I would urge you only to be more-so -- that is, to initiate as well as respond. To notice who isn't here and not assume why, but to check on them; to drop in, to strike up a conversation. To go public. I suspect that, to some degree at least, the camaraderie, kindness, and particular expression of God's Grace that so clearly exemplify this place might be Hart's "Best Kept and Secret" and my hope would be that this place and its way of expressing faith in our Lord Jesus would become Hart's "Wonderful Discovery!"

Thank you, again, for your ongoing friendship with John and me. I thank God for you.
Pastor Shirley Heeg

October 2014
Encountering the bottom line:

In 1521, Martin Luther was called before the Holy Roman Emperor, Charles V to recant to beliefs he had expressed and written in several books that were displayed on the table in front of him. Instead of doing what was expected of him, once again Luther insisted on the authority of the bible over the declarations of popes and councils, clearly implying that human leaders are fallible. Not a popular statement! Tradition tells us he concluded his speech by saying, "Here I stand; I can do no other. God help me."

His stance is impressive, but his demeanor also challenges us, doesn't it? When talking to people who do not share my point of view, I'm pretty sure my impatience or frustration leaks through. Or worse, bursts through! (It has happened!) I think most of us would rather avoid unnecessary disagreements if possible. Being calm and reasonable is hard. Standing on principle takes integrity, but doing it with calm resolve requires another level of Christian maturity.

Each October as Reformation Sunday approaches, I'm reminded that standing for something is necessary. I can still hear my father saying, "If you don't stand for something, you'll fall for anything."

And then there's 1 Peter 3:15, summarizing both the need to take a stand and the best way to do it. *"But in your hearts revere Christ as Lord. Always be prepared to give an answer to everyone who asks you to give the reason for the hope that you have. But do this with gentleness and respect."*

How about you? How would you put the reasons for your faith choices into words? I've given that some thought once again, and here's where I stand on the role of the church today.

To the spiritual-not-religious who ask me why I stay with the church:

Yes, I'm religious. Each time I come to worship, I hope to be religious all the way, straight through to spiritual. That is, I use the words, the prayers, the songs as a threshold, a way to enter the spiritual. And it's a particular "spiritual." The spiritual we enter here is a relationship with the almighty God who remarkably seeks us out, knows us by name, fills us up, confronts us, calls us out, and offers us a panoramic view of life that's wide, healthy, meaningful, and integrated.

I wonder how those of you who are spiritual-not-religious discover that you are valued and loved just for being you. I wonder how life becomes purposeful for you other than managing to stay on top of things. Do you see spirituality as an escape when life gets too demanding? Does your spirituality offer hope and even an eagerness for what lies ahead? What relieves your fears?

I concede that people in churches harm each other, put others off, fail often and a lot. Yet, in every church, every single one, there are some irrepressible souls who "get it." And when you've met them, you know you're in the presence of something other-worldly. They are more than just good people. Where are the persons whose lives have become exemplary by being spiritual-not-religious?

Along with all spiritual people, it saddens me to see lives that are driven. Driving is exhilarating until something breaks down or ages. While all spiritual people admit this, the church takes an additional rather unpopular stance. For Christians, rest means more than retreat, more than distancing yourself from pressures. An honest reason for avoiding church, I suppose, might be that we begin with brokenness and that's something most of us would rather not admit or deal with until we have to. Still…when we do, the grace of our Lord Jesus is so amazing!

So, God help me, I stand in a longing place because I urgently want something for others. I think I understand where Paul is coming from when he writes to the church, *"I pray that you, being rooted and established in love, may have power, together with all the Lord's holy people, to grasp how wide and long and high and deep is the love of Christ, and to know this love that surpasses knowledge—that you may be filled to the measure of all the fullness of God."* (Ephesians 3: 18-19)

Come to church. Sit with me. Let's pray. Let's spread out our thoughts to reconsider them in the light of the sanctuary. Read with me. Consider this lineage of people in the bible who encountered God during their lives, who walked with Jesus, who have sought the counsel of his Spirit. Feel the water. Remember the taste. Leave some things behind. Go in peace.

Pastor Shirley

November, 2014
"Thy Kingdom come on Earth…"   Imagine…

    The breeze is stiff and chilling and surprises us as we round the front of the quaint old seaside shops. Sheltered so convincingly from the wind, we're almost taken aback. We carry a picnic and have come looking for a table. We take each other's pictures, grinning against a backdrop of horizontal rails and mast spires. We're visitors, an odd assortment. John smiles from South Africa, Teri poses in her vivid yet demure Indian sari, Kate seems so young in jeans and a jacket, and I, more motherly in my baggy blue sweater.

    We split up. John and Kate keep to the walkway while Teri and I investigate the shops. We're even different as shoppers; I scan while Teri focuses. Soon, following our instincts, we wander apart. When I step back out into the sunlight between buildings again, I find John and Kate seated at a stone table near a small fountain surrounded by pigeons and sparrows, listening to a rag-tag guitar player.

    We wonder aloud about Teri and two of us go to look, but return without her. We worry a bit now and anxiously search the crowd for her face. Some people come to toss folded bills into the singer's open guitar case and he works "thank-yous" right into his songs without missing a strum. Kate tosses bread to the sparrows and they flit and hop to peck it up. One pigeon is getting its feet washed in the claw-deep water bubbling down behind the singer. While we are thus distracted, Teri has silently returned. She's standing before us with packages in both hands. "See?!"

    Here is a woman in a fur, and there, a boy in a bicycle helmet. Some have nautical parkas; some, business suits. The singer knows all the songs, but we only know a few. The others know those we've missed because of our upbringing. We sing when we know and listen when we don't. All in all, it becomes one fine sharing – lapping and pecking, lyrics and wings, wrappings and breezes – a "now" from many lives, a "here" from many places.

Later, returning to Kate's place for hot tea, I hear her little daughter at the kitchen table singing, "Good news; good news. Good news; good news. Good news, the Lord has come. Good news, the Lord has come." She's making a paper cut-out and now and then she drops the scissors abruptly to unfold and lift another chain of paper people linked hand in hand. But all the while she's examining her work, she continues to sing. 'Why doesn't she end the song?' I wonder; yet, I know she's so rapt in her activity that she doesn't even notice she's singing.

The Kingdom of God is like a marina netting peoples, world, and time into a fine catch. It's coming together after having strayed apart, missing and finding, converging on closeness through gathering and eating, waiting together, and singing.

The Kingdom of God is "Good News, the Lord has come" rattling around in your memory, caught from a child, drummed into your subconscious so surely that it brightens your tired eyes, and permeates your concerns, choices, and hopes.

The Kingdom of God is something different you see in what's right in front of your eyes. The Kingdom of God is something different you do with what's in your hands. The Kingdom of God is something different you catch onto because of what's been given to you.

Pastor Shirley

AMONG US

"Among Us" is a church devotional I wrote to be sent out weekly during the seasons of Advent and Lent for a couple of years. The title is drawn from John 1:14, *And the Word became flesh and dwelt among us....*

These devotionals coordinated with worship texts during those times, but more than that, they sought a connection between our daily lives and the presence of God among us.

Among Us...

A Lenten Meditation, week 1: Reading John 15:1-11

Every Sunday before worship as Nancy plays her prelude, I sit down and bow my head to pray. The very last thing I see before I close my eyes is the stained glass window across from me and every Sunday, for as long as I can remember, I have thought about that window as I formed my prayer. My "prayer window" holds up to the light a beautiful cluster of grapes with a healthy green vine entwined around a communion cup. And, inside, I hear the words of John 15:5, "I am the vine and you are the branches. Those who abide in me and I in them bear much fruit, because apart from me you can do nothing." And inevitably I pray about my own clinging to God in this hour of worship. I love that passage from John, but it troubles me too. Almost every alternating verse makes me terribly uncomfortable. There are the "abide" verses that promise everything from much "fruit," God's love and joy to "whatever you ask" (v. 7), but there are also the pruning, withering, gathering, and burning verses that imply dire consequences. Clearly, dormancy is not an option. When we connect with Jesus, we are supposed to be alive and growing and showing it. Alive with words, alive with love, alive with glad thankfulness to God.

I had a plant once that I thought was alive... that is, until I disturbed it. It looked green and stood upright so I moved it to the bright windowsill where it could be in the light. As I did, it crumbled beneath my touch. Sometimes I worry about having that effect on people. But the truth is with Jesus there is no pretending. Either we connect in a real way or we wither. And how do we begin to connect? Just come.

A Lenten Meditation, week 2: Reading John 10:1-10.

The other day I phoned a woman from the church and although I thought I'd identified myself when she answered, either I had said my name too quickly or didn't say it after all. In any case, she didn't know who I was for a moment--just a fraction of a moment actually. But in that split second of time, we might as well have been strangers. I could clearly hear uncertainty in her voice and in the silences between us, wondering whether or not to answer the question I had asked, wondering who was requesting this information, wondering whether or not to trust and open up to me. But then she recognized my voice and that made a world of difference!

The voice you can trust is the most beautiful of sounds, I think. And your own name spoken by someone who loves you, although it may be heard often enough to be taken for granted, surely is, when considered, one of life's most cherished moments. Perhaps that's why when Jesus wants to describe his relationship with those in his care, he says that they "hear his voice" and that "he calls his own ... by name." I think, no matter what our age, we all long to be cared for in such an attentive and personal way. And any one of us might add: Tuck me in. Comfort me. Lead me gently home. But most of all, don't fail me or trick me because I so need someone I can trust.

Jesus knows that we have times of uncertainty, that we've been hurt and betrayed often enough by others to become wary. But for those who know him, who belong to him, hearing the love and reassurance in Jesus' voice once again makes all the difference in the world! Come and hear.

A Lenten Meditation, week 3: Reading John 8:31-36

I first heard the beautiful harmonies of South African freedom songs at seminary where African students gathered to sing of home. From the beginning I couldn't help but be drawn to the fervent trust expressed in these hymns as well as their hope of freedom. One song praises our risen Lord Jesus who frees those who are held captive and gives bread to the hungry. Suddenly it became clear to me that for these young people captivity meant cold, iron prison bars and hunger, a real ache in the pit of their stomachs. To me, however, captivity is "feeling" trapped, and hunger, something I have around 4:30 in the afternoon if there isn't a snack handy. I guess I stand puzzling with the Jews in this passage when they ask Jesus, "We ... have never been slaves to anyone. What do you mean by saying, 'You will be made free'?"

The answer, of course, has to do with truth and deception. Freedom is knowing the difference. Yet, to be perfectly honest, slavery is just another notion to me, not something I have experienced myself. So I wonder if I can feel the impact of Jesus' words as they whip past me as much as others do who have actually felt welts rise on their own backs.

A slave has no choice, no options, no security. A slave to sin cannot get away from sinning and at any time may be cruelly sold down the river. Perhaps, in my world, the biggest deception, after all, is that such descriptions are gross exaggerations. How bad can sin really be? Can't we just resolve to be better people, more considerate, less selfish, much as we might resolve to diet and reduce the weight we put on from all that late afternoon gluttony? Do we really need someone to set us free? Maybe Jesus is just an encouraging coach or good example -- You know, "If I can do it, you can do it."

"Slave," says Jesus (and he says it to people who think they're already free.) "If I make you free, you will be free indeed!" Come, hear, and be set free.

A Lenten Meditation, week 4: Reading John 12:1-8

We live in a world which prioritizes sight and sound. "Videos" entertain us. Music surrounds us whether we're in the dentist's chair or grocery shopping. I suspect we give much less attention to our sense of smell and, yet, aromas have a wonderful capacity to bring back memories, don't they? I remember sinking into my father's leather chair as a child, for example, and the scent of leather still takes me wondrously back. So I imagine precious memories lingered in the fragrant air for hours after Jesus left his friends' home in Bethany that week-end. Just as they finished supper the last evening they were together, Mary had gone to her room and returned with half a pint of nard, an expensive and heavily aromatic ointment. Impulsively she poured it out on Jesus' feet and then, even more rashly, she loosened her hair and dried them with the long stands. (Immediately Judas had objected, ostensively as an advocate for the poor, but as John points out, really because it galled him to see the fortune that might have come into his own hands draining away at Jesus' feet instead.)

Then Jesus says something peculiar. He implies that Mary, unknowingly, has held onto this oil precisely for this moment, that her generous and loving gesture, in fact, has unconsciously anticipated his death. I wonder if she puzzled over these strange words later that evening when brushing her tresses, no doubt, revived the fragrance. Or as the evening breeze curled through the quiet house soaking up the scent, bringing it to her attention once again. She had merely intended to show how much he meant to her, how thankful she was for their friendship. He had been touched and pleased. She could rest. And as he fastened his sandals the next morning, did Jesus, also, catch the scent? Was it, for him, a reminder of both love and loss, of why it was necessary for him to step into Jerusalem's trap?

There's a message in the air here for us too, I think. When you love someone, you show it. You pour it out; you give yourself up. Christianity is about relationship. Does our love for Jesus move us to worship? Or are we merely interested in what's in it for us? Come, hear, be set free, and worship.

A Lenten Meditation, week 5: Reading John 13:1-5

Passover -- the ancient festival celebrates God's deliverance from death. First in Egypt, the Israelites had prepared a meal of lamb and unleavened bread, painting lamb's blood on their doorways so that death would pass over their households as it moved across the land to claim the lives of all the first born. By the mark of this blood they were saved and Pharaoh was persuaded to let them be free at last. One spring generations later, Jesus himself gathered with his friends to celebrate the ancient meal. But on this occasion new dimensions would be added to the ancient story.

Each Passover has the same ritual. Early in the meal the host washes his hands to signify his position, but, instead, this evening, Jesus rises from his meal and assumes the most humble role possible -- washing the disciples' feet. Wine is always poured four separate times during the meal. The first instance commemorates God as creator-provider. On this night when Jesus refers to the "fruit of the vine," he says he will not drink it again until God's kingdom comes (Luke 22: 17-18). Later in the meal he takes the particular cup recognized by Jews as the cup of redemption and claims that it signifies a "new covenant" marked by his own blood (1 Corinthians 11:25). The Jews have long recalled their years of slavery and bitter tears by breaking bread and dipping it into bitter herbs or a red mixture of fruit and nuts to remind them of the clay that they had been forced to make into bricks for Egyptian architecture. When Jesus dipped the bread, he gave it to Judas who, in just a few hours, would betray him.

And so the meal continued that evening. No doubt the disciples knew the meaning of the passover by heart and surely they sensed that profound changes were taking place. Those who were present then eagerly re-told the event later to others as Christians in the early church shared a similar meal to celebrate their freedom from sin and death through Jesus' crucifixion and resurrection ..

And now -- still more years later -- the traditions come to us. This week we have an opportunity to experience what all of these who have gone before us have known. A mystery. "Very truly, I tell you, whoever believes has eternal life," says Jesus. "I am the living bread that came down from heaven. Whoever eats of this bread will live forever" (John 6: 47,51). Come, hear, be set free. Worship, and remember.

Among Us...

– "NOT SO FAST"–
TRAVELING THROUGH ADVENT

A Meditation for Advent 1: Reading Isaiah 64 – 65

The car actually slowed down for me so I could finish crossing Courtland Street! I couldn't believe it! For as long as l can remember. I have always walked fast. When I first carne here, someone remarked that I came down the center aisle during the last hymn at such a clip that my stole flew out behind me. But today

I'm shuffling and everything seems like a long distance or a great effort. My lower back is clenched with muscle spasms. Now. hobbling back to my car to drive home and get some rest, I think, 'Surely I'll be as good as new in no time.'

But not so fast. Wait a minute. Or rather, many minutes, many hours, and then, several days of barely being able to move. Just last Sunday. someone whose words I value had said, "Shirley, you're such an idealist!" I am. To me, that's what a pastor does among us; she envisions what God's kingdom will one day be and brings that to mind again and again as we live together. Yet, my friend did make me stop and think. So that evening I prayed that I would be more in touch with reality in order to be more relevant and helpful. When I was flat on my back two days later, the sermon topic I'd chosen for Sunday's service seemed ironic: Hope in the Hurts. Reality certainly had settled in and I could have pointed to the very spot it had settled, if it didn't hurt so badly to reach!

Pain and the Sunday when we begin to look forward to Christmas -- what a strange combination, I thought at first. Yet, while reading this week, I discovered that the root of our word "patience" is "patior" meaning "to suffer." And I began to wonder how often in life does waiting for something good to come along really mean waiting for something bad to be relieved?

Isaiah writes of a people who can't find God if their life depends upon it and who are beginning to vaguely fear that it does. Consumed by their own concerns and accomplishments, they have carelessly stretched and torn the ligaments of their lives until now they are gripped with emotional and spiritual pain. However, those who choose to return to God hear this promise: "I...will delight in my people; no more shall the sound of weeping be heard...or the cry of distress." Perhaps one way to wait for Christmas is to get in touch with the painful realities of our own lives and to hear God's words from that position.

A Meditation for Advent 2: Reading Matthew 1:18-25

A situation had developed, one that would take some real figuring to work through. Just when everything had seemed so perfect too. He had finally managed to scrape enough together to set up business in a small shop on the back street and to convince Mary's father that he would be a good provider. Then they had officially announced their engagement! A waiting period was customary. 'Waiting won't be too difficult, 'though,' he had thought. 'It's only a matter of time.'

But not so fast. Wait a minute. That had been yesterday; today everything's changed. Mary's pregnant, she says. And, just like that, it has to be over between them. He'd been thinking about this all afternoon, turning it over in his mind, looking at it from every angle, trying to smooth the appearance
any way he could as if his marriage were a work-in-progress there on the carpenter's bench in front of him.

But no matter how skillfully he tried to re-shape it, the knotty problem wouldn't be straightened out. "I'm a man of integrity," he said out loud. "I have to live what I believe. And yet, I don't want to put Mary through public disgrace." So finally, he had decided. He would quietly arrange for her to go away somewhere. It was the only rational answer. No doubt that decision was difficult for Joseph, but, in the end, he was a man who relied on his good sense. His solution was both reasonable and caring.

That's why I'm surprised by what the angel says that night, aren't you? Why tell Joseph not to be afraid? This isn't your standard angelic "Fear not" greeting, although if we read it quickly, we might be apt to think so at first. No, the angel isn't saying not to be afraid of suddenly seeing an angel like himself appear, but rather, specifically that Joseph isn't to be afraid to take Mary as his wife. Afraid? Is Joseph making this decision out of fear? To himself, as well as to us, Joseph sounds rational, not afraid.

How many times have you struggled with the in's and out's of a problem all afternoon, only to be left with the nagging

149

impression that although the answer you've arrived at seems sensible, it isn't right? Do we, perhaps, try to sound most rational to ourselves and others when really, deep inside, we're afraid?

Maybe Joseph's experience calls into question some of the rationalizations we make as Jesus' birth approaches too. Like, maybe, the reasons we don't want to try to get along with old Uncle so-and -so at the family Christmas gathering any more. Or, why we can't give more to those who are in need. Or, our attitude toward others in the church that, perhaps, keeps us from joining in as we otherwise might.

"I've got my principles and they're good ones, no one can argue that they aren't," I may say, almost out loud. "Besides, it would be too embarrassing now." To such reasoning, the message of God replies, "Don't be afraid to live the way I want you to live. It's a good life with purpose. Trust me. I'm with you."

Joseph had the courage to change his decision. Do we?

A Meditation for Advent 3: Reading Luke 1:45-56

Magazines in racks at the checkout counter always catch my eye while I'm waiting to make my purchases. Even before the stores have begun to dangle red and green honeycombed paper bells from the ceiling tiles above my head or to trail cellophane garlands and pretend snow along their window sills, these magazines anticipate the coming holidays with plates of Christmas cookies or warmly decorated country homes on their bright covers.

But not so fast. Wait a minute. That's not all. Along with their very appealing pictures these covers also name the titles of the most significant articles they include. And lately I've noticed that lots of these articles really are made up of one sort of list or another; have you noticed that too? There are titles like "100 Gifts You Can Make in an Evening" or "50 Gift Ideas for Under $10" – lists for those who are willing to give of themselves, but within reasonable limits. Then, maybe "15 Ways to Eat Well At Holiday Parties and Still Stay Slim" sort of lists for the wishful thinkers among us. Or the "10 Ways to Reduce Holiday Stress" lists so we all survive to begin the new year in some semblance of good health.

That last title piqued my curiosity enough to warrant thumbing through to find the article itself. What advice could lift the spirits of even-busier-than-usual people, I wondered? Had the writer of the article discovered something new?

Eagerly I read the list: "Meditate" was one of the first suggestions. The author elaborated saying that when meditating, it isn't necessary to get in touch with your inner self or anything beyond yourself; in fact, all you need to do is to breathe slowly and consciously. Another suggestion is to "Play" which, he went on to explain, means to break some rules and do something risky. There were others, but as I read on, I couldn't help but think how our holiday Scriptures might sound in terms of such a list.

In particular, I thought of Mary's first Christmas survival list, the one she might have left at her cousin Elizabeth's house for her to consider.

"Meditate," Mary might have begun. Meditate on God! Meditate on what a marvel it is that almighty God has noticed someone like yourself and then marvel all the more that this God has not only noticed, but also reached out to do 'great things' for you!

"Take joy," she, no doubt, would have continued. Take joy in God's mercy for those who suffer and especially in the dependability of God's promises!

Mary's list goes on, but I can't help but recognize that while our modern lists focus on ourselves, hers keeps pointing me to God. And, surprisingly, this young woman, Mary -- whose normal life has been disrupted forever -- doesn't sound as if she is struggling to cope against the odds, to find some way to minimize any possible negative outcomes, or to cut her losses and get through. No, Mary is in this wholeheartedly, trusting God and relaxing in that trust. What good, inviting Christmas traits to adorn our lives as well!

A Meditation for Advent 4: Reading Isaiah 9:2,6; Luke 1:31-33

To and from. I've been filling out a lot of those little labels lately to stick on packages I've wrapped for someone. To Grandpa and Grandma, From John, Shirley and the children; To John, From Shirl; To my teacher, From Meri. So it struck me that this Old Testament passage comes with the same sort of tag attached: To us, From God.

But not so fast! Wait a minute. That's not all. While I take great pains to wrap my presents so no one will guess what's inside, God seems to have a different technique. In fact, when Isaiah writes, many generations before the birth of Jesus, he not only says that this gift is intended for God's people, he also tells us what to expect! Our gift is a child, a Son who will be the "wonderful Counselor, Mighty God, Everlasting Father, the Prince of Peace."

Surely the Israelites who first heard this claim were looking for relief from their oppressor and enemy, Assyria. They needed a flesh-and-blood deliverer, one with amazing qualities who could put an end to their suffering and enslavement and restore real peace! To them God will send a child, one who is both gift and gifted: an amazing child, a God-child, at the same time a flesh-and-blood hero. Even when God plainly tells them what to expect, who can take this in?

Eventually these Israelites are led into peace of a sort; yet, long after they have passed away, still other enemies arise to threaten their children and their children's children. Always the struggle persists. Always it continues because, you see, these battles are only the visible symptoms of an invisible disease. But, wonder of wonders, the promise continues too! It is still extended. It still applies. To you, Israelite tribes who hear the ancient prophet cry out these words in a language we would not understand today.

To your children who long for relief in their time as well. To us, To our children, From God.

Extended across these generations, extended into the depths of our muscle and marrow where this disease has settled -- perhaps now we can begin to grasp why this child comes with such sweeping titles. God wants to assure us that this gifted child is a fitting match for our enemy.

What do you give people who have nothing? You give them everything, of course!

Among Us...

THE ROCKS OF LENT
A Lenten Meditation, week 1: Reading Acts 26:9-18

"Caught between a rock and a hard place" -- the old saying describes how tense and difficult life can seem to us at times, doesn't it? Each of these next few weeks for the children's message during worship we will be adding another stone to our rock garden at the front of the sanctuary and, as we do, we will be taking a closer look at some of those rocky parts of life and what we can learn from them. But, at the same time, through our scripture lessons for worship each week we will be studying the promises of God.

What in the world do rocks and difficulties have to do with God's promises? A great deal, actually. They are a good match because through-out history the church has been proclaiming that the old saying doesn't have it right after all. That when it comes right down to it, our lives aren't really "caught between a rock and a hard place," but rather between a rock and God's promises. That when we are up against it, we can choose to go it alone (doing it the hard way) or to trust in God's loving provision and care.

If that's so, why would anyone choose the hard way? It's a good question. In fact, it's just what Jesus asks in this passage: "Saul, Saul, why do you persecute me? It hurts you to kick against the goads" (verse 14). He's saying, in effect, 'You're being as stubborn as an ox that kicks out at the prod used to guide and move it along. And, worst of all, you're only hurting yourself.'

Yet, until that very moment, Saul didn't see it that way at all. If he thought he was 'hurting' (literally, "persecuting") anyone, it was Jesus, not himself. He never even dreamed that he was hurting himself. You see, Saul had become very good at running down the church, at cutting off its leaders and frightening the others into silence or hiding. He has had the upper hand, the last word, until he comes face to face with Jesus. But Jesus doesn't debate Saul; Jesus doesn't get revenge. Instead, Jesus' heart aches because Saul is destroying himself.

All of which makes me wonder tonight about the opinions I'm so sure of and the arguments I use to put others in their place. Can the church only be the church the way I see it or else be dead wrong? Do I listen and learn from the faith of another or am I quick to squelch others with what I already know? Do I recognize that my own attitudes can destroy me? Can I imagine that Jesus loves me enough to stop me in my tracks when I need it? Am I teachable?

That last question is an important one because Lent, traditionally, is a time of teaching, of learning about ourselves and our relationship to this Lord, Jesus Christ, of learning His purpose for our lives. In these weeks before Easter, consider trusting God's love and leading more fully. You'll find it isn't as hard as you might think.

A Lenten Meditation, week 2: Reading Romans 7:14 – 8:1

As we wake up each morning and get out of bed, John and I are usually preoccupied with what the day ahead holds in store for us. Do you find yourself doing that too? We think about returning to work left undone from yesterday, of new tasks that we have to get to today and we wonder what surprises will come along. Sometimes we feel a heaviness with all of this. That's because, I think, sometimes we have put off what is hardest to face, perhaps hoping that it will fade away or get lost in the shuffle. Sometimes we do what makes us feel good right now, even though we know that it isn't good for us in the long run. At the end of the day, then, lying there in the dark, we can have some regrets about our choices. Why did I say THAT? Why didn't I start earlier? How will I make it up to him? What in the world was I thinking?

Lent is a time of introspection. Yet, when looking into our motives and choices feels dark and discouraging because we seem to repeat old patterns with little or no real improvement over a period of time, we hear Paul describe much the same experience. "I do not understand my own actions. For I do not do what I want, but I do the very thing I hate" (verse 15). This is self-destruction. The "rock" we are coming up against, in this case, is our own self.

What do we do when we are angry at ourselves? What do we do when nothing we try seems to make a lasting difference? "Who will rescue me from this body of death?" cries Paul in deep distress. And the very next words out of his mouth are, "Thanks be to God through Jesus Christ our Lord!"

Jesus saves us even from ourselves! "There is therefore now no condemnation for those who are in Christ Jesus," he continues. No condemnation.

Once when I was a girl I spilled my mother's bright red liquid rouge on the white throw rug in her bedroom. I knew I shouldn't have been playing with it and I was instantly overwhelmed with anxiety about what I had done. I worried about the mess, about the loss of the amount I had spilled, but mostly about being punished for my snooping disobedience. But, wonder of wonders, my mom didn't punish me. She didn't make me clean it up. Instead, she took the loss and cleaned up my mess herself. No lecture; no condemnation!

As I grew up, I went on to do other things that could bring me guilt and shame to think back on even now, but when that greasy, indelible red stain comes to mind, so, too, does the overwhelming relief that I felt when my punishment was set aside! And I know how Paul's mind could jump from his discouragement with himself to such an exclamation: "Thanks be to God through Jesus Christ our Lord!" I've been there.

It's only because we have this promise in Christ that we dare take a good long look at our lives. Otherwise the truth is too painful, too devastating to see. That's why so many people either avoid or deny the consequences of their choices. But "in Christ" we not only see the truth about our inner selves, but also the truth about our salvation. That can make all the difference if we let it.

A Lenten Meditation, week 3: Reading Luke 19:41-44

As we finish eating supper and begin to clear the table each night, like many of you, we turn on the evening news to hear what has happened across the world. Tragedy after tragedy parades before our eyes: tragedy punctuated with popping gunshots from the streets of the West Bank, tragedy accompanied by deep, almost sub-human-sounding moans from Sarajevo where the bodies of children lie in rows in a make-shift morgue, tragedy in stifling silence from the prison cells of dissonants. And everywhere the people weep. They weep and they moan as we clear the table.

And sometimes we weep too. We weep because we are moved with compassion. We weep because we are frustrated by the immensity of these problems and the persistence of evil. And in sober tones, we talk with one another about what should be done. What can be done? Here, too, we enter into mental debate, at times being convicted of the need to act, and at times feeling defensive. Although they don't feel good, such weeping and such conversations are the beginning of compassion, aren't they? And, surely, to respond in compassion is to be like our Lord.

We read of Jesus, "When he saw the crowds he had compassion on them," Mt. 9: 36, "He had compassion on them and healed them," Mt. 14.14. And again, "He saw a great throng and had compassion," Mk. 6:34. "And when the Lord saw her, he had compassion on her and said to her, 'Do not weep.'" Luke 7.13. Time and again, Jesus reaches out in compassion to touch and feed, to heal, and to comfort those in pain.

When Jesus entered Jerusalem those last days of his life here on earth, we read these words about his own compassion: "And when he drew near and saw the city he wept over it, saying, 'Would that even today you knew the things that made for peace! But now they are hid from your eyes,'" Luke 19:.41- 42. Jesus weeps, but Jesus' tears, in this instance, are not for the poor, not for those who suffer under oppression and injustice. No, here Jesus' tears are for the self-confident people of the city. He weeps for their blindness, their indifference to the truth, their callousness to their own responsibilities. He weeps because they are not moved.

Isn't this exactly where God has placed us on this globe, here on the hilltop overlooking our own self-serving and often indifferent culture, our own callous society that hears but does not respond by changing ourselves? Our tears for the world should not only be tears of empathy, but also tears of repentance. How do we move our own peoples to join with all peoples in seeking a more just and peaceful world? The task frightens us, doesn't it?

Jesus looked over the city and wept, then he went down into that city and gave his life. In no other time have people heard the cries of those across the earth as clearly as we do. We have seen their suffering with our own eyes. What if these people could look into our lives? Would they wonder how far we will follow our Lord?

A Lenten Meditation, week 4: Reading Ephesians 5:15-17

Now and then I get a little cynical about my lifestyle. But before anyone is tempted to jump in here with some good advice, I have to be honest and admit that my cynicism isn't just about my own personal schedule of activities, but also about everyone's around me as well. That is, I'm cynical about the way all of us spend our time. I raise the question at home often. Are you too busy? Do you have time to pray, to dream, to reflect about what you're doing and what it all means? Do you? Do I?

Tonight as I left the house to drive back to Hart for an evening meeting, my mind was already racing ahead to the agenda the committee would be covering. Then gradually, as I drove east, I began to notice a brilliant orange reflection in the windows of the houses I was passing. I glanced back through my rear view mirror to see the most gorgeous sunset I can ever remember seeing! And once again, I was struck with the same concern. Is it worth keeping on top of my busy schedule if it means almost missing such a remarkable moment? (Warning: A too-quick answer here isn't very wise either. The better answer may not be what you first assume.)

"Redeem the time," the author of Ephesians writes to the early church. But this isn't merely encouragement to "take time to smell the roses," as one might guess at first. To redeem isn't to relax. It isn't even prioritizing reflective time over action. To redeem is to buy something back in order to save it from being lost forever, to snatch my opportunities eagerly before they pass me by. Opportunities for what? Opportunities to "learn what is pleasing to the Lord" (see verse 10 in this same chapter) and then to live my life accordingly. And, what's more, to do this with a sense of urgency, as if it were of highest importance, even as if it were absolutely essential! Here Christianity isn't a peaceful retreat; it's vigorous and intentional activity.

So the message here isn't 'slow down' or 'take a break,' as we might assume, but rather make sure that whatever we're throwing ourselves into is good and healthy and will please God. After all, how much of what we do each day is primarily designed to get ourselves ahead? And what about FUN? Does it have to be racy? While WE might express personal concerns about the pace of our lives and regret that we are so driven, it seems that God is more concerned about which direction we are moving. Maybe it's high time we traveled toward the light.

A Lenten Meditation, week 5: Reading Luke 22: 24-27

Years ago when I was first married, I remember visiting one of my sisters-in-law only to find her lying on her back on the floor with her little daughter. They were having a great time looking at the underside of the living room coffee table together. "Would you have guessed that there were words scribbled underneath here where the wood is unfinished?" she asked, dusting herself off as she got up to greet me. "No," I replied, but then I had to admit that I couldn't recall the last time I had looked at the bottom of a coffee table or any other piece of furniture or major appliance either. You see, I had grown up.

It's strange, isn't it, that as adults we have given up such child-like things as checking out what the world looks like from the floor up, while at the same time we have retained other childish things like squabbling over who is most important. "Wait a minute," you might object. "When have we ever argued about who's most important?"

When was the last time you (or I) interrupted someone in mid-sentence? Doesn't that say 'my words are more important than yours'? When did we last raise our voices to make a point? Louder is more important. Have we ever listened with our arms folded across our chest, rejecting- everything we're hearing without even considering it? Have we ever quietly resented the attention someone else was getting? Have we ever envied their success? Isn't that just saying, "I should be recognized as that important too"?

Well, at least we're not alone. At their last supper together with Jesus, the disciples begin to do the very same thing. In fact, they aren't nearly as subtle as we have learned to be. "A dispute also arose among them, which of them was to be regarded as the greatest," writes Luke. Jesus mediates their disagreement, but not by weighing the merit of the cases they were making for themselves. Instead, he up-ends the whole conversation and flips

160

their values upside down, saying, "Let the greatest among you become as the youngest."

Self-importance is a stumbling stone to living faithfully. It's good to know what "important" looks like, but only because then we can define ourselves differently. To serve someone else is to demonstrate through our actions just how important that other person is to us. Jesus has shown us how God values our lives by being among us "as one who serves" (v. 27). And that means looking at things differently. For example, who would walk across the street for this squabbling bunch of ungrateful companions, let alone stagger up a hill with a cross beam lashed to your shoulders?

SOMETIMES we're hard on each other. SOMETIMES we're difficult to live with. That's because ALWAYS we're only learning to be what God has called us to be; we're still unfinished. Yet at the bottom of it all, Jesus loves us and serves us in spite of the way we insist on looking at things. I wonder, after all, if that's what is written on the underside of the table.

A Lenten Meditation, week 6: Reading Matthew 26. 36-39; John 17. 20-26

This will be the last of our "Among Us ... " mailings for this Lenten season. It's also Holy Week. Surely this final message ought to reflect the gravity of all that, I thought. But what comes to mind and just won't go away is the punch line of a joke a friend of mine told me a while ago. Something about "Unconverted Rice." And the joke was a play on words, imagining rice grains, each living it up in one way or another. Lots of fun, probably more fun than the converted variety. Shows our assumptions about our being converted (or Christians). To be converted, these grains of rice would have to look a whole lot more serious, wouldn't they? Maybe with halos? Silly? Does conversion mean that our behavior should change? Yes, but maybe not in the way we assume. Yes, but maybe that's not the whole picture. Yes, and more! The pun is that it leaves things at the external level. But

Christianity doesn't end there. It actually doesn't even begin there. What God wants from us isn't just better behavior. What God wants is our hearts! What happened that week long ago? Was Jesus' death an automatic fulfillment of the ancient promises, all pre-programmed, holy "behavior"? The church calls this time the "Passion" of our Lord Jesus. And surely passion refers to his suffering on the cross, to being "forsaken" by God as he pays the penalty for our sin, but his passion also begins before those last hours. Jesus' passion can be heard in his struggle of will and devotion. In his commitment. In his trust.

Matthew recounts Jesus' words to his disciples on the night before his death, "My soul is very sorrowful, even unto death." And then his words to God in prayer, "My Father, if it be possible, let this cup pass from me; nevertheless, not as I will, but as thou wilt." (Mt. 26. 38, 39b) John recalls yet another prayer on that evening, this one for the disciples themselves and for us as well, "That they may be one even as we are one, I in them and thou in me, that they may become perfectly one, so that the world may know that thou hast sent me and hast loved them even as thou hast loved me," (John 17.22b-23).

It's an excruciating time for Jesus, but the reason for his passion -- the outcome he asks for -- is that we might all be ONE. Nothing less. Not just that we should get along better with one another after this. Not merely that our lines of communication be kept open. To be ONE. That we find the very meaning of life "in" God and one another. Earlier Jesus had described it this way: "You shall love the Lord your God with all your heart and with all your soul and with all your mind ... and ... you shall love your neighbor as yourself." (Mt. 22.37, 39)

What Jesus did in those last hours was to live this from the inside out. He didn't just go through the motions for us. No, he allowed his heart to be crushed. Does Jesus' passion move us? Does it bring each of us to ask, after all, if our own heart may yet be the stone left unturned?

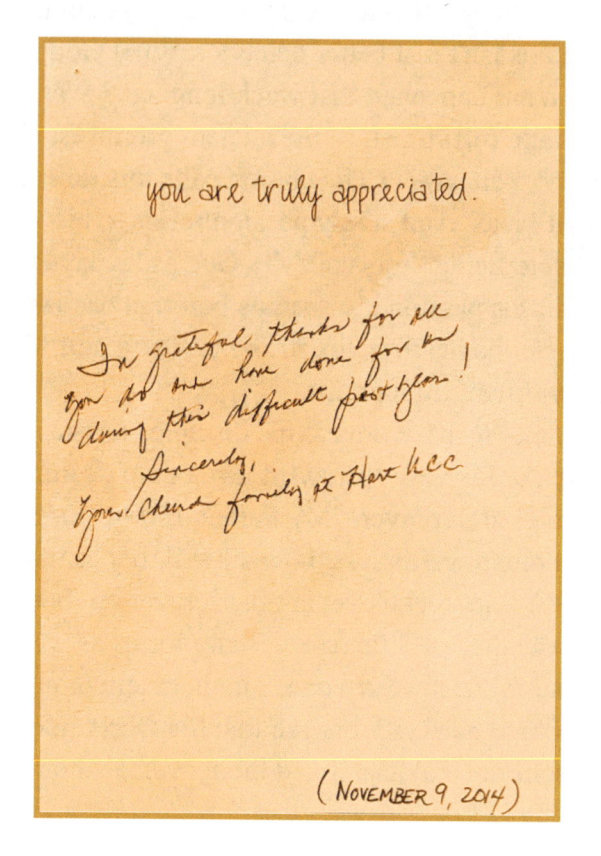

CONCLUSION

A year after I had returned to HUCC, the congregation decided to explore the possibility of sharing a minister with the UCC church in Shelby. It was time for me to leave once again. It was difficult to walk out of the building, but I knew that, for me, Hart Congregational UCC was always going to be more of a time than a place. I loved people who were no longer there. I grieved when I left the first time. I was with them when they grieved the loss of their next pastor. Then I grieved when I left the second time. As it is written in calligraphy on the staircase railing at the church, "Life doth have its ups and downs."

And yet, *The light shines in the darkness, and the darkness has not overcome it.* (John 1:5)

The "light" in this for me is that the past doesn't change. Yes, the future is uncertain, but maybe not as much as we might assume. I trust and watch for goodness to show up again on the path ahead. We know, don't we, that through it all, God continually provides out of such a great love for us?

Surely, I am with you always. (Matthew 28:20)

Ahh, amen.   SH

NOTES

*pg.6, encounter, V. (1). *Webster's New World Dictionary of the American Language, College Edition,* World Publishing, 1962, p. 478.

WORKS CITED

Newspaper clippings from Oceana Herald Journal on pp. 5, 59, 106, 112, 116, 117, used with permission of editor, September, 2023.

Scripture references from NRSV, RSV, or NIV, editions of Thomas Nelson Publication Bibles, Zondervan, and are used here under their Gratis Use guidelines.

Scripture reference from *The Message*, quoted within guidelines from NavPress Publishing Group.

Other works cited are in public domain.

Made in the USA
Columbia, SC
24 May 2024